101 WAYS TO
IMPROVE
BUSINESS
PERFORMANCE

101 WAYS TO
IMPROVE
BUSINESS
PERFORMANCE

DONALD WATERS

**KOGAN
PAGE**

To Michael and David

First published 1999

Kogan Page Limited
120 Pentonville Road
London N1 9JN

© Donald Waters, 1999

British Library Cataloguing in Publication Data

A CIP record for this book is available from the British Library.

ISBN 0 7494 2981 X

Typeset by Kogan Page Limited
Printed and bound in Great Britain by Clays Ltd, St Ives plc

Contents

CONTENTS

CONTENTS

Introduction

Last year Lloyds TSB put £102 million into their employees' profit-sharing scheme; two directors of Selfridges shared a £62,000 performance bonus; Misys announced record profits and their share price rose 17 per cent in a day; McDonald's celebrated its 25th birthday by giving two Big Macs for the price of one; Jenny Beaumont got £2,500 from her company's productivity improvement scheme. It's good news when your company does well. You congratulate yourself on a job well done – and are rewarded by pay, promotion, status, praise and anything else that's going.

If, on the other hand, your company does badly, competitors circle around like vultures, swooping on any chance of taking your business. So improved performance brings the benefits of:

- long-term survival;
- achievement of objectives;
- less waste and lower operating costs;
- a competitive advantage and higher sales;
- better financial results, such as higher profits, income and wages.

At this point you are probably asking three questions. Firstly, what do we really mean by 'performance'? There are hundreds of answers to this. You could, for example, measure sales, market share, profit, value added, return on investment, output, productivity, quality, unit cost, customer loyalty, staff morale and so on. In this book we don't rely on any specific measure of performance, but concentrate on the underlying operations. The way to increase market share is by making a better product that customers want; the way to reduce operating costs is to use a better process.

Secondly, you might ask if the same methods work in every organization. In practice, managers face common problems, whether you work in Nissan, Great Western Trains, Charnwood

1

Borough Council, or Fred's Diner. High productivity and low operating costs are – like apple pie – always good; falling sales and low morale are – like sin – always bad. In this book we stick to general principles that you can use anywhere.

The third question asks how you can improve performance. The next nine chapters give 101 ideas for this. These are not quick fixes that claim dramatic results with virtually no effort, but they are real methods that are used in organizations around the world. Some of them are difficult and need a lot of work – but they can give huge, long-term benefits.

The methods are based on the principle that every organization makes a 'product' that satisfies customer demand. This product is a combination of goods and services – like SupaSnaps where the film processing is a service and the photographs delivered are goods. Each product is made by a specific process. This is true whether you work for a manufacturer, service, government, charity, trust, social club or any other type of organization.

As a manager, you are responsible for every aspect of your organization's performance. You make the decisions, design the systems and control the results. If the organization does well, it is because of your efforts. This book describes some practical ways of ensuring good results.

Managers and Decisions

Managers are paid to make decisions. You decide what your organization does, who works there, what they do, how and when they do it and everything else about the operations. This is a difficult job. As Anthony Robbins says, 'If making decisions is so simple and powerful, then why don't more people follow Nike's advice and "just do it"?' (Robbins, 1991).

You are totally responsible for your organization's performance. If you do a good job the organization thrives; if you do a bad job... well, you'll find out fairly quickly. This chapter makes some general points about your job as a manager and what you can do to improve your organization's performance.

WAY 1   MAKE DECISIONS

As a manager, you spend your time:

- *planning* – setting goals and showing how to achieve them;
- *organizing* – designing the best systems to achieve the goals;
- *staffing* – making sure there are people to do all the jobs;
- *directing* – guiding and coaching employees;
- *motivating* – empowering and encouraging employees to do their jobs well;
- *allocating* – assigning resources;
- *monitoring* – checking progress towards the goals;
- *controlling* – making sure the organization keeps moving towards its goals; and
- *informing* – telling everyone about progress.

It is difficult to be a good manager. You make decisions in complex situations, with rapidly changing conditions, uncertain goals, little information, tight deadlines, external constraints that you can't control and uncertain relations with other people and organizations.

Some people have a habit of making awful decisions. Other people avoid decisions by delaying work until it is too late, always demanding more information, finding more important things to do, forming committees, avoiding contacts, or passing the decision to someone else. We all avoid difficult jobs – which is why 1.1 million people were late returning their income tax forms last year. But managers are paid to make decisions – and if you don't, you are not doing your job. If you can't dance, get off the dance floor.

So your first job is to recognize your role in setting the organization's performance, be positive about making decisions, be decisive and be committed to the results. Lee Iacocca gave the advice, 'When it comes time to make decisions, you shouldn't get too old over them. Sure, they won't all be perfect. In fact some of them will be duds. Learn from them, but don't stop trying' (Iacocca, 1988).

In brief

As a manager, you are responsible for the performance of your organization, and must make the necessary decisions with confidence and enthusiasm.

WAY 2   TACKLE DECISIONS PROPERLY

Most of us think that we are good at decisions. Mention a problem in a pub, and people will happily tell you how to solve it – as well as every other problem that humankind has ever faced. Unfortunately, the reality is that we jump to conclusions, are inconsistent, have preconceived ideas, are prejudiced, use wrong assumptions, ignore available information, lack experience, don't have enough knowledge and simply make mistakes.

To make good decisions, you have to approach them properly. The first step is to analyse the situation. You make a decision when you have a number of different courses of action and must choose the best. After making your decision the future unfolds – but you have little control over this – and eventually you gain the rewards. This is like betting on a horse race; you look at the alternatives and choose the best horse; then the race is run, but you have no control over the winner; finally you see the results of your decisions.

You need a way of consistently choosing the best alternative. Paul Sharman of Focused Management Information says that managers 'evaluate the facts and consider the alternatives; discuss the facts and alternatives with people whose opinion the managers value; and finally, managers go with their gut instinct'. A better approach has the following seven steps:

1. Describe the problem – finding the exact problem, its cause, the context, effects, seriousness and variables.
2. Define your objectives – showing what you want to achieve, and giving priorities to different objectives.
3. Collect and analyse data – getting all the relevant information.
4. List all the alternatives – including those which are not immediately obvious.
5. Compare the alternatives and find the best – examining the consequences of each alternative, and finding the one that best achieves your objectives.
6. Implement the decision – doing whatever is needed to carry out the decision.
7. Monitor progress – checking what actually happens over time and making any adjustments or new decisions.

Problems are not easy to solve – or they wouldn't be problems! Perhaps the most common fault is jumping at the easiest or most obvious solution. If a decision is at all important, you should approach it carefully and spend the time necessary to find the best solution.

In brief

Don't leap into decisions, but use a considered approach that gives consistently good results.

WAY 3   TAKE RESPONSIBILITY FOR YOUR DECISIONS

Even the best decisions are no use unless they are implemented. This implementation needs a combination of communication, persuasion, commitment and ability – and you can only get this when everyone is convinced of the benefits.

Of course, we all make mistakes, and what seems like a good decision at one point can turn out to be a disaster. You don't have to look far to find embarrassing mistakes like the Ford Edsel, IBM's PCjr, Coca-Cola's new formula, the Hunt family's investment in silver which lost US $2.5 billion, Concorde, Gerald Ratner's description of his products as 'absolute crap', and so on. When this happens there is no point in trying to deny it, hide the facts, or pass the blame to someone else. As Ken Iverson said, 'You have to have a strange and monstrous ego to think that you never make bad decisions' (in McCormack, 1995).

In 1997 Assim Computers made record profits, and the senior managers awarded themselves a large annual bonus. In 1998 economic problems in Asia caused intense competition, falling prices, overcapacity and declining sales. Assim Computers made an operating loss and their share price fell by 65 per cent – but the managers felt that they had still done a good job in saving the company from bankruptcy, and awarded themselves the same generous bonus.

This kind of crooked reasoning – where good performance is due to good management, but poor performance is due to factors you can't control – doesn't convince anyone. It only encourages distrust, bad feelings, conflict and dishonesty. You should make the best decisions you can, and then accept responsibility for them. As Maria O'Connor of Ticketmaster BASS said, 'Make the hard decisions first. Just make a decision! But I think the biggest one is, to take responsibility for what you do.'

In brief

Even the best decisions can go wrong. Accept responsibility for mistakes and learn from them.

WAY 4   GIVE DECISIONS THE ATTENTION THEY DESERVE

Clive Ponting describes how the government's decision to spend £10 billion developing the Tornado aeroplane was made in two minutes in a Defence Committee meeting. This speed is a marked contrast to the long debate in Cabinet about whether they should send the Russian Ambassador a Christmas card (Ponting, 1986).

Some decisions are important to your organization, with effects over many years; other decisions are less important, with effects over days or even hours:

- *Strategic* decisions are the most important ones made by senior managers; they give general guidance for the whole organization over the long term, use many resources and involve high risk.
- *Tactical* decisions are the less important ones made by middle managers; they give more detailed direction for parts of the organization over the medium term.
- *Operational* decisions are the least important ones made by junior managers; they give detailed instructions for each operation over the short term, use few resources and involve little risk.

Organizations need decisions at all levels, and you should give each decision the amount of attention it deserves. You only have a limited amount of time – and if you waste this deciding whether to have tea or coffee, you won't have enough left over to make the decisions that are really important.

I once attended a meeting with 63 other people (not an ideal number for making fast decisions!) and there were 18 items on the agenda. After three hours we were still discussing the first item. The meeting had to end and the rest of the items were carried over until a later date. But at least we had decided that the chairman no longer had a reserved parking space near the door – if he wanted the best space he should arrive at work first. Unfortunately, the trade union that threatened industrial action had to wait for their answer, as did the German company that was considering a strategic alliance.

In brief

Give decisions the amount of effort they deserve, and don't get bogged down in detail.

WAY 5   CONCENTRATE ON YOUR CORE FUNCTIONS

If you have a simple question about planning permission, it is very difficult to find anyone in your local council who can answer it. To an outsider, councils and most other organizations are horribly complicated. But this hides the fact that they all have a simple purpose – to supply products that satisfy customer demand. Colin Marshall of British Airways summarizes this by saying that, 'The simple principle is that the company exists to serve its customers long into the future.'

The most important activities in your organization are those which are directly concerned with satisfying customers. In IBM these activities make computers; in Barclays they give banking services; in Safeways they sell food. You should put all your effort into these central activities – which are usually described as the three core functions:

- *Sales/marketing* – identifies customer demand, stimulates new demand, collects customer information, organizes advertising, takes orders, etc;
- *Operations* – actually make the goods and services;
- *Accounting/finance* – raises capital, invests funds, collects money, pays bills, maintains accounts, etc.

You can probably think of a long list of other activities, such as research and development, human resource management, information systems, administration and public relations. But you can either include these supporting activities in one of the core functions, or they are not directly concerned with products and customers.

Every organization has to do the core functions. If you don't make a product, sell it and organize the finances, you won't have an organization to worry about. But you can put different efforts into each one. Carlsberg brewery puts more effort into marketing, but it still needs to control its finances and have efficient operations; Royal and Sun Alliance emphasizes its finances, but it still needs efficient operations and marketing. The only way of improving performance is by concentrating on these core functions, and doing them better.

In brief

There are three core functions involved in supplying a product. You can only improve overall performance by doing these core functions better.

WAY 6   CONCENTRATE ON THE VALUE CHAIN

The three core functions are part of a cycle for satisfying customer demand:

- *customers* demand
  - *products* which are made by a
    - *process* which consists of
      - *operations* which give the
        - *finished products* which are sold by
          - *marketing* and distributed to
            - *customers.*

You can only improve performance by improving the core functions. To be more precise, you have to concentrate on the activities that form this cycle. These are the activities that add value, generate income, satisfy customers, create wealth and achieve all the other objectives of your organization. They are the heart of your business. As Ernst and Young say, 'All companies... have a heart. Everything else is a sideshow' (Ernst and Young, 1992).

Activities that are not part of this chain are an overhead that you can reduce or eliminate. Remember that your organization is not there to occupy a beautiful office block, or give you a company car, or provide a child-minding service. It is there to satisfy customer demand as a way of achieving its objectives. As John Egan of Jaguar cars said, 'The absolute fundamental aim is to make money out of satisfying customers.'

Michael Porter (1985) expands the operations part of the cycle to focus on five elements:

- research and design;
- development;
- production;
- marketing and sales;
- distribution.

He said that you can create and sustain a competitive advantage by concentrating on these areas. To be successful you have to excel in at least one of them.

In brief

Concentrate on activities that form part of the value chain, and which satisfy customer demand.

WAY 7   MEASURE YOUR ORGANIZATION'S PERFORMANCE

You should monitor your organization's performance to make sure that it is going in the right direction and is moving with reasonable speed. More specifically, you monitor performance to:

- see how well the organization is achieving its goals;
- compare the organization's current performance with its performance in the past;
- compare your performance with other organizations;
- compare performance in different parts of the organization;
- make decisions about alternative investments;
- make decisions about changes and measure their effects;
- help with internal functions, such as wage negotiations;
- highlight areas where performance should be improved.

Sometimes you can only give a subjective view of progress, saying that 'morale has improved' or 'the new designs are a distinct improvement'. It is much better to use a quantitative measure, saying that 'we sold 240 units last month'. This gives an objective view of performance and, as Lord Kelvin said, 'When you cannot measure it and express it in numbers, your knowledge is of a very meagre and unsatisfactory kind.'

Almost every organization measures profit and productivity, but there are hundreds of other measures ranging from long-term debt ratios through to short-term machine utilization. Each of these looks at a different aspect of operations. So by collecting a series of different measures you can monitor different aspects of progress. When you see that sales rose by 10 per cent last year, your celebrations might be diminished when you find that profit fell by 20 per cent.

To get a broad, overall view of the organization you need a 'cock-tail' of different measures. Glen Penwarden of Orillia Soldiers' Memorial Hospital in Ontario said, 'Approximately 100 of the numerous key result measures developed by our departments and programmes were selected for monitoring at the corporate level.' Remember that 'what you can't measure, you can't manage.'

In brief

Monitor your organization's performance, using a cocktail of quantitative measures.

WAY 8   CHOOSE THE RIGHT MEASURES

You can measure performance in hundreds of different ways, including costs, turnover, profitability, return on assets, share price, earnings per share, price to earnings ratio, number of employees, capacity, resource utilization, efficiency, sales per employee, market share, number of customers, value added, fixed costs, customer loyalty, staff turnover, etc. Some of these are much easier to find than others. But you should not use measures simply because they are easy. If, for example, you have a high staff turn-over – more than 10 per cent a year – you should measure morale, even if this is rather difficult.

A reasonable measure of performance:

- is directly related to your goals;
- shows how well you are achieving these goals;
- focuses on significant factors;
- is directly measurable and uses consistent units;

- is objective;
- allows comparisons of performance;
- is agreed by everyone concerned.

Remember that each measure describes only one aspect of the organization. In January 1999, Hollinsco had 10 people organizing 1,000 life insurance policies a month for high-risk travellers. In February the company did some reorganization, and then employed 11 people who organized 1,200 policies – but direct costs had risen from £55,000 to £102,000. Table 1.1 shows two measures of performance.

Table 1.1 Measures of performance

	Before reorganization	After reorganization
Number of policies organized per person	1000/10 = 100	1200/11 = 109
Direct costs per policy	55,000/1000 = £55	102,000/1200 = £85

The productivity of each person has risen, but so has the direct cost. Whether the reorganization was a success depends on Hollinsco's objectives. If increased capacity was wanted then the reorganization was a success: but if reduced unit costs were wanted it was a failure. You will always find such contradictory views of performance. When you drive a car faster the time needed for a journey goes down, but the fuel consumption goes up; when you reduce the selling price of a product, the demand goes up, but the profit goes down; when you reduce bonus payments, the wage bill goes down, but so does productivity. You should keep your overall aims in sight, and use the measures that show how well these are being achieved.

In brief

Use measures of performance that are directly related to your organization and its aims.

WAY 9   USE BENCHMARKING

Absolute measures of performance often have little real meaning. You may be interested to hear that Long Rock Agricultural Merchants have annual sales of £400 per square metre, but you don't know how good this is until you compare it with results from other stores. Measures of performance give the clearest results when you use them for comparisons. You can get the standards for these comparisons from four different sources:

- Absolute standards give the best performance that you could ever achieve, such as zero defects or 100 per cent utilization.
- Target performance is a more realistic level that is agreed by managers, who set a tough, but attainable, target.
- Historical standards look at performance that was actually achieved in the past, so this is the worst performance you should accept.
- Competitors' standards show the performance being achieved by competitors, so this is the lowest level you must reach to stay competitive. Federal Express delivers packages 'absolutely, positively overnight' so Tufnell's Big Green Parcel Machine must deliver 'next day guaranteed'.

Benchmarking compares your organization's performance with a competitor. To be blunt, you use benchmarking to find ideas and methods that you can copy. By looking at your competitor's operations, you get realistic performance targets, and see how to achieve them.

You can use any organization for benchmarking, but it makes sense to use those which have the industry's best performance. Unfortunately, it can be difficult to get information from them, so you have to use other organizations that are willing to share ideas. Sometimes it is worth looking at completely different types of organization – so Great Western Trains can learn something from bus operators, airlines, or other companies that give high customer service, such as supermarkets.

Then the benchmarking process is to:

- decide the process to benchmark and the best measures of performance;

- find the competitors with the best performance and collect data on their operations;
- compare operations, find and analyse differences;
- see why the competitors' operations are better and look for ways of reaching the same standards;
- redesign your own operations to bring performance at least up to the standards of the best competitor;
- implement the changes;
- monitor progress, make necessary adjustments and continue benchmarking.

Many organizations still have a 'not invented here' attitude. Benchmarking takes exactly the opposite view and recognizes that other organizations have very good ideas that you can adapt and adopt.

In brief

Benchmarking looks at the best performance achieved in your industry, and shows how you can match this performance.

WAY 10   FOCUS ON CUSTOMERS

Without customers you have no sales, no income, no profit, no business – and soon no organization. Unfortunately, when you meet other managers they often seem to forget this, and talk about profits, productivity, return on investment, debt ratios and personnel problems. Sometimes customers are clearly an irritant, getting in the way of smooth operations, asking awkward questions and making unreasonable demands.

Perhaps I should say yet again that the purpose of your organization is to supply a product that satisfies customer demand. This should be the focus of the whole organization. As Michael Perry of Unilever says, 'To sustain competitive advantage requires a total commitment to your customer', while Glen Penwarden of Orillia Soldiers' Memorial Hospital says, 'If it is good for your customers, do it! The dollars will follow.'

This concentration on customers involves:

- finding out exactly what customers want;
- designing products to meet these demands;

- doing research and development so that your product range responds to changing demands;
- aiming for complete customer satisfaction;
- getting a reputation for outstanding quality and value;
- doing after-sales checks to make sure that customers remain satisfied;
- looking outwards so that you are always in touch with customers, potential customers, competitors, alternative products, etc;
- allowing customers easy access to your organization and making them welcome;
- discussing customer service widely, so that everyone knows your aims, and shares thoughts on customer satisfaction.

Some people say that you should go further than merely satisfying customers, and should exceed their expectations – delighting or cosseting them. As Tom Farmer says, 'At Kwik-Fit we're committed to delivering 100 per cent customer delight.' Whatever you call it, you depend on satisfied customers coming back with repeat business. It typically costs five times as much to attract a new customer as it does to retain an existing one – and someone who gets good service will recommend you to four or five other people, while someone who gets poor service will warn a dozen potential customers to go somewhere else.

In brief

Concentrate on customer service, supplying products that satisfy their demands, and preferably exceed their expectations.

WAY 11   WELCOME CHANGE

You work with continuous change. Products change – as do competitors, costs, markets, locations, customers, the economy, the business environment, company objectives, technology, shareholders, employees and just about everything else. If you don't respond to these changes, your organization will decline as it gets left behind by more flexible competitors. Some of the signs of a decline include:

- old products that are being overtaken by competitors;
- low sales volume and falling market share;
- problems with product quality and delivery dates;
- large numbers of customer complaints;
- reliance on a few customers, especially with long-term, fixed price contracts;
- an old-fashioned process;
- low employee morale and high staff turnover;
- poor industrial relations;
- poor communications;
- too much, inflexible, top management;
- inward-looking managers who are out of touch with operations or customers;
- heavy debts.

John F Kennedy said, 'Change is the law of life. And those who look only to the past or the present are certain to miss the future.' Unfortunately, most of us don't like changes. They force us to abandon old and familiar practices, to learn new skills, new ways of doing things, new procedures and to form new relationships. These are difficult, and you may feel that change is inevitably for the worse – 'improvement always means deterioration'. But you should recognize that change is inevitable and is a normal part of business. To be more positive, you have to welcome change as it creates opportunities, gives improved conditions, operations, performance and rewards, with more interesting and secure jobs. This constructive attitude involves:

- commitment to change, accepting that continual change is inevitable, necessary and beneficial;
- a business culture and environment that welcomes change;
- an experimental approach, encouraging new ideas and practices;
- products and operations based on innovation and new ideas;
- keeping abreast of new developments and likely changes in the industry;
- acceptance that not all new ideas will be successful, and willingness to learn from failures;

- easy communications, so that everyone knows about the changes, why they are needed, their effects, new practices and so on;
- reassurance, guidance and protection of people most affected by changes;
- managers who enjoy change;
- introduction of changes steadily so that they are easily absorbed, rather than making a dramatic response to a crisis.

In brief

Continual change is inevitable. You should positively encourage change and welcome the opportunities it brings.

WAY 12   INTRODUCE CHANGES PROPERLY

While welcoming change, remember that there is no point in making changes for change's sake. Remember that 'to change and to change for the better are two different things'. One notorious change for the worse was Coca-Cola's decision in 1985 to improve their 100-year-old formula. After intensive consumer research, they replaced the old formula by one that customers consistently preferred in tests. The result was tonnes of letters from dissatisfied customers, and 1,500 complaining phone calls a day for three months. Within two months the company decided to return the original formula as 'Coke Classic'. Roger Enrico of Pepsi-Cola was obviously delighted, saying, 'This was a terrible mistake.'

The moral is that you have to change for a reason, go in the right direction and introduce the changes properly. You might use the following steps:

1. Make everyone aware that changes are needed, describing the reasons, alternatives and likely effects.
2. Examine the current operations, using benchmarking and other comparisons to identify areas that need improvement.
3. Design better operations using the knowledge, skills and experience of everyone concerned.
4. Get people committed to the new methods.

5. Design a detailed plan for introducing the improvements, anticipating likely problems rather than waiting for them to happen.
6. Make any changes to the organization.
7. Do the training and education.
8. Set challenging, but realistic, goals for everyone, and make it clear how these can be achieved.
9. Have a specific event to start the new methods.
10. Establish milestones and monitor progress to make sure they are achieved.
11. Give support and encouragement to everyone concerned.
12. Have continuing discussions about progress, problems, adjustments, etc.
13. Remain committed to the new methods, updating them as necessary.
14. Accept that the new methods are only temporary, and continually look for further improvements.

In brief

Make changes for a valid reason, and then introduce them properly.

WAY 13 MAKE NOTES OF POSSIBLE IMPROVEMENTS

It is easy to get so involved in your business that you don't see the wood for the trees. You spend so much time working with the present systems that you don't have time to think about better ones. If you sat back for a few minutes you could probably think of hundreds of improvements – Why is my computer at this angle? Why is the receptionist so scruffy? Why have we hired more people to look at our overstaffing problem? Why don't we contract out catering and transport? Why doesn't someone open a 24-hour shop nearby? Why don't we sell in Canada? What exactly does that department do?

You should give yourself some time and note down ideas for making things better. Don't worry if these make sense, but think about them and see how you can develop them in the future. Here is a quick list to help you on your way:

- contract-out peripheral jobs;
- dispose of unused capacity;
- cut back on obvious waste;
- hold managers responsible for excess costs;
- simplify administrative systems;
- reduce the amount of paperwork;
- automate administrative systems;
- don't collect information that you don't use;
- use data mining;
- use activity-based costing;
- use management science;
- be prepared to take some calculated risks;
- always have contingency plans;
- don't keep managers behind closed doors;
- manage by walking about;
- close the executive dining-rooms;
- keep meetings short;
- use management by objectives;
- set clear, numerical targets;
- encourage creativity;
- generate new ideas by brainstorming;
- encourage internal promotions;
- review the staff appraisal schemes;
- get a better employee suggestion scheme;
- help poor performers to improve;
- develop people's skills;
- don't allow delegation upwards;
- use zero-based budgeting;
- investigate declining performance;
- set clear priorities for expenditure;
- don't have too high specifications in materials;
- use value analysis for materials;
- negotiate better terms from suppliers;
- delay payments for as long as reasonable;
- hire or lease instead of purchasing;
- use preventive maintenance;
- tighten credit allowances;
- renegotiate loans;
- improve your price structure;
- eliminate unprofitable activities;
- redistribute resources to increase returns;
- avoid high-cost projects;

- eliminate small and unprofitable accounts;
- keep promised deadlines;
- use more efficient transport;
- make better use of storage space;
- use control charts to identify poor performance;
- publicize achieved performance;
- use information maps;
- keep a business library;
- don't use 'it's company policy' as an excuse.

In brief

There are many ways of improving performance, but you have to generate ideas and find the time to develop them.

Think Strategically

This chapter talks about the long-term, strategic decisions that set the overall direction of your organization. This gives your organization its purpose and objectives, and shows how you will achieve these. As Alvin Toffler said, 'A corporation without a strategy is like an aeroplane weaving through stormy skies, hurled up and down, slammed by the wind, lost in the thunder heads. If lightning or crushing winds don't destroy it, it will simply run out of gas' (Toffler, 1985).

WAY 14   TAKE A LONG-TERM VIEW

I assume that you want your organization to stay in business for the long term. If this is true, you have to design a strategy that gives it long-term aims and shows how you will achieve these. If there is no strategy, the organization will drift along without any sense of direction or purpose. As Laurence Peter said, 'If you don't know where you are going, you will probably end up somewhere else.'

ICI made a strategic decision to move out of bulk chemicals and into consumer products, so it sold its bulk divisions and bought Unilever's Speciality Chemicals (for $8 billion), Acheson Industries, Williams Home Improvement, National Starch and so on. The strategy of Jennifer Penhaligan is to expand her Rural Theme Parcs, opening one new centre every four years. Sears' strategy concentrated on its core activities of clothes retailing, so it decided to sell all other parts of the business, including William Hill, the British Shoe Corporation, Freemans, Selfridges and Creation (this left it rather vulnerable and the remaining activities were bought by January Investments Limited in 1999).

Unfortunately, it takes a lot of time to design a reasonable strategy, and you have to fit this around your more immediate concerns. If people are hammering on your door, you will deal with them rather than shut them out and think about things that might happen in five years' time.

But strategic planning is essential, and there must come a point when you set aside the day-to-day problems – however important these may be – and concentrate on the longer-term strategy. This can be awkward, but you must do it if you want your organization to survive.

In brief

You must find time for the long-term planning that sets the overall direction of your organization.

WAY 15   DO A SWOT ANALYSIS

You can start your planning with a strategic review to see what the organization is like at the moment. You can summarize this in a SWOT analysis, which outlines the organization's strengths, weaknesses, opportunities and threats:

- *Strengths* show what the organization does well – features it should build on;
- *Weaknesses* are problems the organization has – areas it should improve;
- *Opportunities* can help the organization – openings it should seize;
- *Threats* can damage the organization – hazards it should avoid.

Strengths and weaknesses describe the organization's internal features, and typically include people, products, structure, finances, reputation, processes, assets and knowledge. Opportunities and threats describe external features and typically include the economy, competitors, markets, technology, new controls, laws, external relations, society, the environment and expectations of stakeholders.

Synergistic Consultants have recently done a SWOT analysis. They used brainstorming sessions to collect the views of managers, and then spent some time analysing the results. Their lists started with strengths of expertise, innovation and local contacts;

weaknesses of small size, gaps in experience and local operations; opportunities from the increasing use of information technology, new management methods and new businesses opening nearby; threats from larger competitors, high overheads and a possible takeover. Synergistic Consultants then designed its business strategy around these results.

Some people say that there are really only three strategic questions. Where are we now? Where do we want to be? How do we get there? A SWOT analysis answers the first of these questions, and lays the foundation for the other two.

In brief

A SWOT analysis gives a summary of your organization's current position and indicates the best direction in the future.

WAY 16   DESIGN A MISSION STATEMENT

There are several types of strategic plan, including:

- *mission*, which is a simple statement of the overall purpose and aims of the organization;
- *corporate strategy*, which expands the mission to show how a diversified corporation will achieve its mission;
- *business strategy*, which shows how each business within the corporation will contribute to the corporate strategy;
- *functional strategies*, which describe the strategic direction of each function, including operations, marketing and finance.

Most organizations have a mission or vision, which is a simple statement to summarize the organization's reason for existence. 'The mission of the Institute of Management is to promote the art and science of management'; at Lloyds TSB, 'Our aim is to be the best and most successful company in the financial services industry, a leader in our chosen markets'; 'Marks and Spencer aims to become the world's leading volume retailer with a global brand and global recognition'; 'Tarmac aim to be an innovative, world-class provider of high-quality products and services which add value to our customers in the built environment.'

Some organizations give more details, like ICI who say that:

We intend to be the world leader in the chemical industry in creating value for customers and shareholders – and to achieve it through the following means:

- market-driven innovation in products and services;
- winning in quality growth markets worldwide;
- inspiring and rewarding talented people;
- exemplary performance in safety and health;
- responsible care for the environment;
- the relentless pursuit of operational excellence.

Unfortunately, missions often seem like clichés – always involving excellence, global leadership, outstanding performance and so on. But a good mission statement gives a focus for the organization and a context for all other decisions; it makes sure that everyone is working towards the same aims, that there are no conflicts and that resources are shared out sensibly.

The mission must be flexible enough to allow change. Volvo, for example, say that 'Volvo creates value by providing transportation-related products and service with superior quality, safety and environmental care to demanding customers in selected segments.' In 1999 the best way of achieving this mission was to sell the car division to Ford and concentrate on commercial vehicles.

In brief

A mission gives a statement of the overall aims of an organization, and is the starting point for all other decisions.

WAY 17   DESIGN CORPORATE AND BUSINESS STRATEGIES

The corporate strategy shows how a complex organization achieves its mission – and the business strategy shows how each business within the corporation contributes to the corporate strategy. These strategies typically include decisions about shared values and beliefs; industries to work in; amount of diversification; businesses to start, acquire, close or sell; type of products to make; organizational structure; relations with customers, suppliers, shareholders and other stakeholders; geographical locations; and targets for long-term profitability, productivity, market share, etc.

You should consider three factors when designing corporate and business strategies:

1. The *mission*, which gives the overall aims and context for other decisions.
2. The *business environment*, which includes all factors that affect an organization but which it cannot control, such as:
   - *customers* – their expectations and attitudes;
   - *market* – size, location and stability;
   - *competitors* – the number, ease of entry to the market, their strengths;
   - *technology* – currently available and likely developments;
   - *shareholders* – their objectives, returns on investment, profit levels;
   - *other stakeholders* – their objectives and amount of support;
   - *legal restraints* – trade restrictions, liability and employment laws;
   - *political, economic and social conditions* – including stability, rate of growth, inflation, etc.

The business environment is similar for all competing organizations, so to be successful you need a distinctive competence.

3. The *distinctive competence*, which includes the factors that set your organization apart from the competitors. If you can design new products very quickly, innovation is a part of your distinctive competence; in Rolls-Royce cars the distinctive competence comes from making the best cars in the world; in the Post Office it comes from daily deliveries of mail to every address in the country. A distinctive competence comes from your organization's assets, which include:
   - *customers* – their demands, loyalty;
   - *employees* – skills, expertise, loyalty;
   - *finances* – capital, debt, cash flow;
   - *products* – quality, reputation, innovations;
   - *facilities* – capacity, age, value;
   - *technology* – currently used, planned;
   - *suppliers* – reliability, service;

- *marketing* – experience, reputation;
- *resources* – patents, ownership.

The strategic plans show how the organization can achieve its mission. As Kenneth Blanchard and Spencer Johnson said, 'Take a minute. Look at your goals. Look at your performance. See if your behaviour matches your goals' (1983).

In brief

The corporate and business strategies show how your organization can develop a distinctive competence to compete effectively in its environment and achieve its mission.

WAY 18 USE A SENSIBLE APPROACH TO STRATEGIC PLANNING

You can design strategies in many ways – usually involving a mixture of analysis, reasoning, experience and intuition. One approach looks at the organization's strengths and weaknesses in relation to its competitors. If most of your competitors are making low quality products, a good strategy is to make the best products available. Supermarket chains are building very large, out-of-town stores – so Spar runs small, convenient, local stores; many airlines compete with cheap, no-frills services – so Fairlines International offer an expensive service with very high levels of comfort and luxury.

There are many ways to approach strategic planning. As Gay Gooderham of Doneco says, 'No one "right" way to develop and implement strategy exists. The key to successful planning is to get the best fit between the chosen tools and techniques, the organization's current culture, capabilities and business environment and the desired outcome.' One useful approach has the following steps:

1. Analyse your organization's mission and other strategic plans, to find the context and overall aims of this strategy.
2. Set goals to show the results that this strategy must achieve.
3. Analyse your existing strategies, finding their aims, seeing how well these are being achieved and looking for improvements.

4. Analyse the environment in which your organization works, giving the competitors, their performance, customers, products, etc.
5. Find the factors that will lead to success in this environment, and the importance of each; emphasize the products needed to compete effectively.
6. Describe the approach that will best achieve success; emphasize the process that can best deliver your products.
7. Design the best organizational support, including structure, controls and related functions.
8. Define measures to compare actual performance with planned, optimal and competitors' performances.
9. Implement the plans, setting the aims and conditions for other levels of decisions.
10. Monitor actual performance and continuously look for improvements.

In brief

Strategic planning is a complicated process and you should use a rational approach that will give consistently good results.

WAY 19   DESIGN AN OPERATIONS STRATEGY

A business strategy gives the aims of your whole business. Each of the core functions within the business has its own functional strategy. Operations are the activities which are directly concerned with making a product, and the related long-term decisions form the operations strategy.

The operations strategy gives the link between more abstract business plans and final products. The business strategy describes general aims, while the operations strategy looks at the products and processes which will achieve these. Cadbury have a business strategy based on market leadership in confectionery – and their related operations strategy has large-scale production and distribution of a range of chocolate bars. Southwest Airlines have a business strategy of competing aggressively on price; their operations strategy provides a no-frills, low-cost service using secondary airports, no meals or entertainment and simplified booking.

The operations strategy is concerned with matching what the organization is good at with what the customer wants. It answers questions like:

- What type of products do we make?
- How wide a range of products do we offer?
- What types of process do we use?
- What technology do we use?
- How do we maintain high quality?
- What geographical areas do we work in?
- How can we plan capacity and get economies of scale?

In 1997 the Body Shop adjusted its business strategy to regain some of its dramatic growth of the 1980s. The associated operations strategy included a new store format, new services, expansion of existing overseas markets (which already have 90 per cent of stores), opening in new Asian markets, tailoring products and packaging to tastes in different countries and tighter control of overheads.

Other core functions have their own strategies; these must be co-ordinated to contribute to the overall business strategy. An operations strategy of mass production, for example, must have an associated marketing strategy of mass sales, and a finance strategy of heavy capital investment.

In brief

You must have an operations strategy, which contains all the long-term decisions directly concerned with your products.

WAY 20   DESIGN A MARKETING STRATEGY

A marketing strategy contains all the long-term decisions made for marketing. A traditional view bases this on the 'four Ps' of getting:

- the right Products;
- to the right Place;
- at the right Price;
- with the right Promotion.

A broader view includes decisions about channels of distribution, market segmentation, entry methods, timing product launches, marketing mix and so on.

Marketing encourages customers to buy your products, but customers all seem to want different things. Some people put a high price on image and buy Calvin Klein jeans, while others are interested in value and buy Eastern Butterfly jeans. Every decision to buy a product has two stages. The first stage finds a short list of products that have all the 'qualifying factors'. These are the features that a product must have before customers will even consider buying it. Public transport, for example, must be fast, convenient and cheap, or people will not even think of using it. The second stage looks at 'order-winning factors', which are the features that identify the best product from the short list. If several computer systems have all the qualifying factors, price and speed might be the order-winning factors that decide which one you buy.

Your marketing strategy aims at delivering products that consistently have the qualifying factors, and score well with order-winning factors. There are two ways of doing this: *cost leadership* makes comparable products more cheaply; and *product differentiation* makes products that customers cannot find anywhere else.

Lyons Bakeries are cost leaders who make standard cakes so efficiently that their unit costs are low; La Patisserie Française use product differentiation to make different types of cakes with much higher prices. You might think that a compromise between cost leadership and product differentiation gives the benefits of both strategies. But this does not seem to work, and you get stuck in the middle making average products at average prices.

In 1983 Kelloggs' share of the US cereals market had fallen to 37 per cent. They responded with an aggressive marketing strategy based on renewed commitment to quality, emphasis on the adult market and a tripling of the advertising budget to around 20 per cent of sales. By 1987 Kelloggs' share of the market had bounced back to 41 per cent. But times change, and by 1999 Kelloggs' share had fallen to 32 per cent of the US market, as customers refused to pay for the huge advertising costs and moved to cheaper brands. Kelloggs again adjusted their marketing strategy to emphasize value, and substantially reduced their retail prices.

In brief

A marketing strategy makes the long-term decisions that encourage customers to buy your products.

WAY 21   CONTROL FINANCES

Goods and services flow from original suppliers, through operations and on to final customers. Alongside this physical flow goes the information you need to manage the operations. In particular, the financial records track the products, show where you earn money, where you spend it and where you make your profits. This financial information helps keep your organization on a sound footing. As Woody Allen said, 'Money is better than poverty, if only for financial reasons.'

A lot of financial controls use simple ratios, like the return on assets:

Return on assets = net income/total assets

You probably use several ratios of this kind, to measure:

- *profitability* – such as return on assets, return on investment, return on equity and profit margins;
- *utilization of assets* –such as asset turnover, stock turnover and collection period;
- *liquidity* – such as current ratio and quick ratio;
- *debt utilization* – such as gearing, debt ratios and interest cover.

Taken together, these measures show how well you are doing the operations. But remember that financial statements are indicators and not ends in themselves. Robert Heller said, 'Businesses and managers don't earn profits, they earn money. Profit is an abstraction from the true, underlying movement of cash in and cash out' (1982).

To improve your financial position you don't juggle figures in the accounts until they look better, but you improve the operations. In 1998 North-Pemberton improved its utilization of a packing machine from 73 per cent to 89 per cent. This gave a healthy improvement in their finances, but the most important point was that they had better control over their operations.

Some organizations are surprisingly innovative in their financial management. The Body Shop, for example, at one point considered moving out of the stock market to become a charitable trust.

In brief

Financial controls give the information which shows how good your operations are.

WAY 22   IMPLEMENT YOUR STRATEGIES

Even the best strategies are no use unless you implement them. So your strategies must be realistic, achievable and beneficial – and you must persuade people that there will be real advantages. The Project Management Group in the University of Southern Alberta had a mission of 'being world leaders in research, teaching and practice of project management'. Unfortunately, there were only three people in the group, and they could never get anywhere close to achieving their ambitions, which were based on dreams rather than realities.

When designing strategies you have to ask the following types of question:

- Do we have, or can we get, the necessary resources?
- What time-scale is involved?
- Do we have, or can we train, people with the necessary skills?
- How will the strategy affect our present and potential customers?
- What are the impacts on staff, facilities, organization, technology, etc?
- What are the overall benefits and risks?

But even if you ask these questions and get the right answers, it can still be difficult to implement strategies. Perhaps the main problem is that senior managers who design the strategies are simply too remote from operations. They see the financial ratios, but have little idea how the organization really works. On the other hand, people working with the details of day-to-day operations have little time for corporate ideals. Lofty aims such as 'being a global leader' have no relevance or meaning. Some common problems with strategies are:

- they are badly designed;
- they are not implemented properly;
- they are not related to actual operations;
- they are not realistic;
- they ignore key factors;
- people only give the appearance of supporting the strategies;
- enthusiasm for the strategies declines over time.

Despite these difficulties, you must implement the strategies, or you have wasted your time designing them. My nephew spent the whole of last summer designing his dream house. Of course, when you're only 10 years old it's difficult to implement such plans – but at least there are no shareholders asking about the waste of time and money.

In brief

Implementing strategies may be difficult, but you have to overcome the problems and give your organization its direction.

Look After Your Most Valuable Asset

Most organizations boast that 'our most valuable asset is our people'. You probably agree with Tesco that 'the quality of our people defines the success of the business'. But the truth is that many companies make a habit of treating their employees very badly. When it's time to reduce costs, companies jump into 'downsizing' or 'rightsizing' – thus getting rid of their most valuable assets, while keeping the office furniture, equipment and other peripherals. As John Harvey-Jones says, 'There is practically no area of business where the difference between rhetoric and actuality is greater than in the handling of people' (1994).

Decisions affecting people in the organization come under the general heading of human resource management, which is: 'a range of strategies, processes and activities designed to support corporate objectives by integrating the needs of the organization and the individuals that comprise it' (Cushway, 1994).

WAY 23   MANAGE HUMAN RESOURCES

Human resource management (HRM) makes decisions about the people who make up your organization. Its range of activities goes from strategic analyses to find the human consequences of the mission, down to routine personnel administration. To put it briefly, HRM integrates the needs of the organization, and of the individuals who form it.

To achieve this aim, HRM:

- analyses the human resource implications of the mission and other strategies;

- designs human resource policies to support the organization's goals;
- provides support and expertise to line managers;
- improves communications within the organization;
- handles any human problems that arise within the organization.

As you can see, HRM likes to emphasize its strategic role, and its responsibility for the most important resource. It emphasizes the view that 'the organization is its people' – and we should all be viewed as assets rather than costs.

You might think of HRM in terms of its more traditional role in personnel management, where it is concerned with:

- job analysis and design;
- selection and recruitment;
- training, development and career planning;
- performance appraisal;
- compensation and benefits;
- retirement and dismissal;
- industrial relations.

Whether it is concentrating on its strategic role, or administering personnel procedures, HRM is crucial for every organization. Careful management here gives you motivated, skilled employees who work hard for the organization. They realize that by contributing to the aims of their employers, they can achieve their own goals. As a simple example, IBM of Canada started a reward-based suggestion scheme, which received 6,000 suggestions in the first year. The company implemented 1,000 of these, gave the staff US $200,000 in rewards, and saved US $4.6 million. Of course, you might question the fairness of a suggestion scheme that gave the company 96 per cent of the benefits and the employees 4 per cent.

In brief

Human resource management must be done carefully as it tries to integrate the needs of your organization and the people who comprise it.

WAY 24   TREAT PEOPLE PROPERLY

It may be a cliché to say that 'a happy worker is a productive worker' – but there is a lot of truth in it. Everyone is more effective when they enjoy work, and no one does a good job if their heart sinks at the very thought of going to work. I once spent a year doing a job that bored me to tears, and I can't think of a single productive thing that I did while there.

We all want to be treated with courtesy, respect and consideration, so an obvious way of improving performance is to treat everyone within the organization in the way that you would like to be treated yourself. You should, for example:

- make sure that people are treated courteously, without favouritism, prejudice, public criticism, malevolent gossip, inconsistent policies or unreasonable behaviour;
- make people feel welcome and comfortable in the organization, with support and good working conditions;
- not use 'macho managers' to make people feel intimidated and insecure;
- give clear job descriptions so that everyone knows what their job involves – and give training, support and guidance so they can do it properly;
- treat people as individuals – design jobs to match their interests and abilities, allowing a sense of achievement;
- show the importance of everyone's jobs and reward them fairly with money, recognition, promotion and other incentives;
- give people responsibility and allow them to make as many of their own decisions as possible;
- set individual goals and make these demanding but achievable;
- measure everyone's contribution, acknowledge these publicly and reward them – making a clear link between performance and rewards;
- encourage teamwork and co-operation, and bring people together to sort out conflicts;
- have direct, open communications, with information flowing freely around all levels of the organization – don't keep secrets from people;

- arrange regular meeting to discuss targets, progress, problems, etc;
- show how progress can be made through a career path;
- measure absenteeism and staff turnover, as these give a clear picture of morale and job satisfaction.

In brief

Treat everyone with courtesy, respect and consideration – as you would like to be treated yourself.

WAY 25   HAVE OPEN COMMUNICATIONS

Information must move freely around an organization. Information about operations must move upwards so that higher managers have the relevant information for their decisions; information about decisions must flow downwards so people know the details and context of their work; and information must flow horizontally so that different functions can be co-ordinated. This seems obvious, but many managers still think that they have to be secretive. During the small talk over coffee I once asked a BBC accountant how much some equipment cost. 'I can't tell you – it's secret,' was the rather stern reply. I wasn't particularly interested, but the details were freely available from suppliers, trade journals, published accounts and many other sources. The accountant was simply trying to maintain his perceived advantage, and build a mystery around some obscure fact.

Unfortunately, some managers hear that 'information is power' and they try to keep their authority by depriving others of essential – or at lease useful – facts. Their formal justification is that information might be misused within the organization, or it might be passed to competitors and other outsiders. These fears are greatly overstated, and the advantages of freer information within the organization greatly outweigh the costs of possible misuse.

If people don't have access to real information, they will make assumptions – and their imaginations can run wild. A reasonable decision to replace a company car after four years rather than three will lead to rumours about falling orders, redundancies and closure. When trust and freely available information are missing, fantasy and fear become the norm.

Factors that encourage good communications include:

- an open business culture with mutual trust and responsibility;
- appropriate means of communications, including written reports, e-mails, informal meetings, etc;
- clear, brief messages using simple language and format;
- honest communications, without lying, being secretive or exaggerating;
- messages tailored to receivers;
- reinforcement to emphasize important points;
- feedback from the receiver to make sure they understand.

You spend a lot of time communicating with colleagues. Remember that there are two reasons for these communications. Firstly, they pass information around: secondly, they maintain personal relationships. This second purpose is often as important as the first.

In brief

Information must flow freely through your organization, or else barriers appear and management becomes more difficult.

WAY 26   MOTIVATE PEOPLE

Management styles change, and the old-fashioned idea of barking orders at cowering underlings has been replaced by discussion and co-operation between colleagues. As Denis Waitley says, 'Yesterday leaders commanded and controlled. Today leaders empower and coach' (1995). This new approach is based on motivation. People don't work because they are afraid not to, but because they positively want to.

Three hundred years ago John Locke said, 'When there is no desire there will be no industry.' So you have to motivate people to want to work. Motivation is difficult to define, but a person is motivated if they keep working hard to achieve a goal. This gives three aspects to motivation:

1. *effort* – a motivated person will work hard;
2. *perseverance* – a motivated person will continue working for as long as needed;
3. *effectiveness* – a motivated person will work towards a goal.

Most people work well if they know what to do and are suitably rewarded. If someone does a job badly, it probably means that they don't know how to do it properly. The easiest way of correcting this is with coaching and training.

Of course, you might not be giving enough rewards for doing a good job. Very few of us would work conscientiously if we had bad conditions, appalling pay and few other rewards. But we would work well if there were things to motivate us, and these come in two types.

Firstly there are external rewards that you get for doing the job, such as pay, status, relationships with colleagues, security, holidays, promotion, praise and work conditions. These are the conditions that must be met by a job, and if they are missing it is difficult to get anyone motivated. Secondly, there are intrinsic rewards that come from how you feel about the job. These are the positive motivators that encourage you to do a good job, and include achievement, recognition, responsibility, autonomy, personal development, interest and satisfaction of doing a good job.

People tend to list the intrinsic factors as reasons for staying in a job, but give extrinsic factors as reasons for leaving. This is why my last assistant left, saying, 'I enjoy the work here but am leaving to get some promotion.'

In brief

You must motivate people to work hard at achieving your organization's goals. Remember the old saying that 'you can manage things, but have to lead people'.

WAY 27   DELEGATE RESPONSIBILITY

Decisions made at different levels in an organization need different information, knowledge, skills and experience. No one can make good decisions at every level, which is why managers concentrate on specific levels. Executives concentrate on strategic decisions that need a broad overview of the business, supervisors look at operational decisions that need a detailed knowledge of the process and so on.

Unfortunately, it is often hard to admit that other people are in a better position to make decisions, and will get better results than we can. But you must delegate decisions to the people who can get the best results – and this usually means that you delegate to the lowest possible level. John McKrindle was proud of his 'hands on' style of managing the family transport company. No one else could make any decision, and it seemed clear that the company wouldn't last long when its indispensable leader died of a heart attack at the age of 42. John's widow appointed a new management team who tripled profits within two years. Nobody is irreplaceable, and other people can make much better decisions than you imagine.

Delegating decisions has many benefits, including:

- allowing personal development and achievement;
- enabling faster decisions to be made close to operations, rather than waiting for decisions from remote managers;
- allowing better decisions by those with most knowledge and information;
- providing more time for senior managers to concentrate on strategic issues;
- entailing lower costs, as decisions are made at lower levels and some layers of management can be removed;
- giving improved customer service, as people who deal directly with customers can solve their problems;
- enabling employees to have more control and responsibility for their jobs;
- offering employees more satisfaction, sense of achievement and commitment;
- permitting release of skills, knowledge and creative abilities of employees;
- encouraging continuous improvement of processes.

In brief

Nobody can make decisions at every level, so you should delegate decisions to the best level, preferably as low as possible.

WAY 28   EMPOWER PEOPLE

Empowerment gives people more control over – and responsibility for – their work. It is based on the idea that those most closely involved with operations are in the best position to make decisions about them. So it delegates responsibility as far as possible, with people using their knowledge and abilities to manage the details of their own job, free from the instructions and control of a more remote supervisor.

You can see the difference when you go into a shop to exchange a shirt. Marks and Spencer has empowered employees, and the first person you meet will happily refund your money or change the shirt as you prefer. In Broadbridge & Co the assistant doesn't have this authority, and passes your request to a supervisor in their head office, who will deal with it when they have time.

There are five main types of management style:

1. I decide and you do – which is the traditional authoritarian approach.
2. We discuss and I decide – which involves some discussion but responsibility remains at the higher level.
3. We discuss and we decide – which is more collaborative and has some real delegation of control, but ultimately authority and responsibility remains with the senior manager.
4. We discuss and you decide – which delegates most control of the decision.
5. You decide and I'll help if needed – where the senior manager hands over control, and acts as a coach and consultant if needed.

The last level is closest to empowerment and is the approach that is becoming more widely accepted. As Bill Gates says, 'Empowering leadership means bringing out the energies and capabilities people have and getting them to work together in a way they wouldn't do otherwise' (Entrepreneur, January, 1994).

Empowerment gives more authority to people lower down the organization, and it also puts more demands on them. They must be willing to accept this responsibility, be able to make good decisions, work without supervision and probably form part of a team which completes an identifiable part of the whole process.

In brief

There are many benefits of empowerment, which passes responsibility for work to the person actually doing it.

WAY 29   FLATTEN YOUR ORGANIZATION

Your organization should have the best structure for achieving its goals. This structure shows the internal divisions of the organization, and the relationships between them. The structure is not fixed, but evolves to meet changing conditions. Unfortunately, this generally means a drift towards more complex structures, with more divisions, extra layers of management, longer chains of command, less delegation and more centralization. Endless levels of management can be used for minor rewards and recognition. Catherine Beresford was very flattered when Pennsylvania Citizen Corporate Bank offered her a job as vice-president – even when she found that she was on the lowest of nine levels of vice-president, along with 482 others.

John Harvey-Jones says, 'Such is the complexity of organizations, that not only do we actually have lots of people who are over us, but most of us are blessed with even more who believe themselves to be over us, and to have endless rights of interference in our business' (1993). The proliferation of management layers is hopelessly inefficient. It forms an army of people whose only job is to force information to travel through a long and convoluted route before it is used, and makes sure that decision makers become hopelessly remote from the operations.

Delegation has clear advantages (see Way 27) and empowerment allows you to reduce the layers of management. So the best type of organization is as flat as possible, with only a few layers of management. As John Browne of BP says, 'The organization must be flat, so that the top is connected to the people who actually make the money.'

Flattening the organization means that each manager becomes responsible for more people. There is a limit to the number of people that one person can supervise, but this span of authority varies widely between jobs. Roman legions used a span of 10 people, but most people imagine that a manager can only handle a few subordinates. In reality, proper delegation allows you a surprisingly wide span, allowing a much flatter and leaner organization.

In brief

Remove all layers of management that are not absolutely essential, and have the organization as flat as possible.

WAY 30   USE TEAMS

Teams are coherent groups of people with complementary skills who work together towards a specified goal. Teams are often the most efficient way of working, and their benefits include:

- the members achieving more by working together than they would by working separately or in large, unstructured groups;
- improved motivation and effort;
- flexibility to deal more effectively with change;
- more imaginative solutions to new problems;
- fewer mistakes, as faults are spotted by other members;
- fair division of work, resources and rewards.

Nelson Mandela asked, 'How can one individual solve the problems of the world? Problems can only be solved if one is part of a team' (1990). Notice that there is a difference between a team and a group of people who are simply working together. A team is a cohesive set of people who are motivated to achieve common goals. Simply collecting different people does not give a team, as they don't trust each other, bring along internal politics, don't share common goals and so on. Remember that 'Twenty people in a room doesn't make a team. Teams don't just happen. They have to be developed, facilitated and motivated' (Kriegel and Brandt, 1996). A successful team needs:

- agreed, common and challenging goals;
- leaders who can unite the team and plot its direction;
- commitment to solving problems and achieving goals together;

- power to make decisions, implement them and take responsibility for consequences;
- active involvement of all members, with clear roles for each;
- mutual trust, open communications and co-operation between all members;
- acceptance of members' differences, with constructive resolution of conflict;
- shared rewards.

Self-directed work teams combine the benefits of teamwork and empowerment. They are autonomous and have full authority to manage themselves and the process they work on. They look at the work to be done, and then schedule their time to achieve this most effectively. There are still team leaders who are accountable for performance, but they are less directors and more co-ordinators and facilitators who give support and guidance.

In brief

Teams are often the most effective way of working, but they have to be properly formed and motivated.

WAY 31   TRAIN AND EDUCATE

Your organization is continually changing, so employees constantly need to develop new skills and expertise. In other words, they need training and education. This seems obvious, but many companies ignore basic training and find the disadvantages of:

- higher costs of recruiting skilled people, rather than training them;
- higher staff turnover as people look for more opportunities;
- less knowledge of organizational objectives, systems, methods, etc;
- worse performance from people lacking necessary skills;
- less flexibility, innovation and ability to change;
- long time needed to learn new methods and procedures;
- more accidents.

At the end of 1998 Jim Baxter was making a lot of mistakes with his orders, and customers were complaining. He wasn't deliberately doing a bad job, but no one had told him how to use the new order-entry system. A two-hour course solved all the problems – leaving Jim, his employer and his customers very happy. Some companies still say, 'We train our staff and then they leave' – to which the obvious response is, 'What happens if you don't train them and they stay?'

When you go into a shop and the person serving is rude, it is probably because they have never been told how to treat customers properly. At the other extreme are companies that put a huge effort into training – and you will never be treated rudely in McDonald's.

If you have empowered employees, it is particularly important to train them. People with new responsibilities must also have the necessary skills and knowledge. This training can take many forms, but typically includes:

- knowledge of the organization, its mission, objectives, culture, systems, etc;
- people skills, including leadership, motivation and team building;
- business skills, including decision making, time management and communications;
- working knowledge of various functions, including finance, marketing and operations;
- specialized knowledge, perhaps in accounting or information systems;
- general knowledge, including health, safety and environmental concerns.

I hope that you don't agree with Oscar Wilde who said, 'Education is a admirable thing, but it is well to remember from time to time that nothing that is worth knowing can be taught.' Allen Sheppard of Grand Metropolitan was more accurate when he said, 'Training should be seen, by employers and employees, as an essential investment with rich returns for both when it is properly focused.'

There's an old story about a manager who makes a really bad decision which costs his company US $10 million. He goes to his boss to explain. The story has two endings. In the first the boss says, 'I wouldn't dream of sacking you – after I've just spent

US $10 million on your training.' In the second ending the boss lifts his telephone and says, 'Send security up to remove this dangerous imbecile.'

In brief

You have to make sure that everyone in the organization is properly trained for his or her job.

WAY 32   DESIGN JOBS

Job design looks for the best way of doing any particular task. It describes the details of the work to be done, the skills and equipment needed, supervision, interactions with other operations, environment and so on. From the organization's point of view, the aim of job design is to make employees productive and efficient. But employees have their own social and psychological needs, and they want to interact with other people, be recognized, appreciated and properly rewarded. So the real aim of job design is to meet the performance goals of the organization, while making the job safe, satisfying and rewarding for the individual.

There are three elements in job design:

- The *physical environment* is the place where the job is done, its layout, the tools used, equipment available, lighting, temperature, noise, safety features and so on.
- The *social environment*, which affects the psychological well-being of the people working. A good social environment gives a higher quality of working life, and leads to higher motivation and better performance.
- *Work methods*, which describe the details of how a job is done. Work methods usually break the job into a series of small tasks and analyses each of these. In particular, they ask questions like 'Why is this task done?' 'What is its purpose?' 'How is it done?' 'Why is it done this way?' 'Could it be done automatically?' 'How could the layout of the workplace be improved?' 'Would different tools help?'

When L&M Industries looked at their process for making window frames, they counted 162 separate steps. Of these, 39 involved walking to fetch materials and tools, and another 18 involved waiting for something to happen. By redesigning the jobs, L&M reduced the amount of movement by 85 per cent and cut the time needed to make each frame by 58 per cent.

Such improvements need someone to recognize that changes are needed and then do the planning. This can take time. In the 1960s a series of armed robberies in Montreal made Canadian banks install a centralized cash dispenser for the tellers in each branch. Then to cash a cheque, you queued to talk to a teller, and then the teller queued to use the cash dispenser. You could still see this laborious system in use long after improved security gave many more efficient solutions.

In brief

You have to design jobs properly, so that they satisfy the needs of both the organization and the employee.

WAY 33   DON'T EMPLOY TOO MANY PEOPLE

This seems obvious; employing too many people to do the work is clearly a waste of money. Unfortunately, there is a natural tendency for organizations to expand – largely because it is easy to employ an extra person, but difficult to sack one. This growth is particularly obvious at the top. I once looked around a department in the old ICI and was surprised at the large number of senior managers. The reason was that they went around other departments to collect information from senior managers, who would only talk to them properly if they were on an equal footing.

Most organizations are overstaffed – perhaps by up to 10 per cent. C Northcote Parkinson says that when someone is overworked they can resign, share the work with a colleague, or demand another two assistants. He adds, 'There is probably no instance, however, in history of [anyone] choosing any but the third alternative' (1957).

When there is not enough work to keep everyone occupied, there is plenty of time to worry, gossip and play politics. This by itself can be disruptive, but there are more problems when you try to trim the costs. Your best people will read the signs and start looking around for another job; the less good will keep their heads down and avoid any controversy, risks or mistakes. No one performs at their best when they spend their time applying for other jobs or trying to look invisible.

Remember that those who are in danger of losing their jobs deserve the longest warning that you can give. It isn't their fault that the organization is having problems, and they have to plan for a difficult and uncertain future. Many managers delay these decisions, giving different reasons why they shouldn't say anything until the last possible moment. This leaves everyone worried. It is far better to sort things out early, so that those remaining can concentrate on their work, and those leaving can plan for the future.

In brief

Overstaffing has more widespread effects than simply wasting money, and you should avoid it by controlling recruitment and promotions.

Focus on Your Operations

Operations are the activities that actually make your product. Ray Wild of Henley Management College describes 'the production/operations function as the core – the essential part – of any business' (1995). The only real way of improving the performance of your organization is by improving the operations. You can set about this in many ways – which is just as well, as there are lots of organizations that need improving! How many times have you looked around and thought, 'They could do things a lot better if they…' There may well be people looking at your operations and thinking the same thing.

WAY 34   EMPHASIZE OPERATIONS

At the heart of every organization are the operations that actually make goods and provide services. To put it simply, the operations describe what the organization does. Operations at IBM make computers; at British Airways they fly passengers; at Royal and Sun Alliance they give insurance; at Rosebury Junior School they educate children.

When you talk about an organization's performance, you are describing how well it does its operations. To improve performance, you have to improve the operations. This seems obvious. But managers often ignore this simple truth and try to find quick fixes that don't involve any effort.

The general manager of Asiatic Pine (I've changed the name for obvious reasons) adjusted the way the annual overheads were divided between production and customer service. Table 4.1 shows the results in thousands of pounds.

Table 4.1 Annual overheads

	Before change	After change
Production	Overheads 50	Overheads 30
	Direct costs 120	Direct costs 120
	Total 170	**Total 150**
Customer service	Overheads 20	Overheads 40
	Direct costs 30	Direct costs 30
	Total 50	**Total 70**

The company made no changes at all to its operations or actual costs, but it seems to get the double benefits of reducing production costs and increasing customer service. You can always juggle the accounts to give apparent improvements, but these are just illusions – all smoke and mirrors. The only real way of improving performance is to do the operations better. Michael Treacy and Fred Weirsema acknowledge this when they talk about three winning strategies, 'product leadership, operational excellence and customer intimacy' (1995).

Always remember that you can do great deals with the finances, spend a fortune on marketing, have the best working conditions, use the latest technology – but if your operations are no good you might as well shut the door and go home.

In brief

The only real way of improving the performance of your organization is by doing the operations better.

WAY 35   USE OPERATIONS MANAGERS

At first sight, the operations in different organizations don't seem to have much in common. British Steel seems completely different to the Crown Inn, Goldsithney. But if you look closer there are surprising similarities. Managers in both organizations find the best location for their operations; they both choose suppliers and buy raw materials; they use a process to turn the raw materials into products; they forecast customer demand and calculate the capacity needed to meet this; they organize resources as efficiently as possible; they are concerned with cash flows, productivity, quality and profit.

In principle, operations in every organization are similar. They take a variety of inputs (such as raw materials, money, people and machines) and do operations (such as manufacturing, serving and training) to give outputs (which include goods, services and waste material):

- Nissan's assembly plant in Washington takes inputs of components, energy, robots, people, etc; its operations include pressing, welding, assembly and painting; the main outputs are cars and spare parts.
- The Lobster Pot Fish Restaurant takes inputs of food, chefs, kitchen, waiters and dining area; its operations are food preparation, cooking and serving; outputs include meals and, hopefully, satisfied customers.
- The Open University takes inputs of students, books, buildings, staff, etc; its operations are teaching, research, administration and service; outputs include better educated people, research findings and new books.

Operations managers are, not surprisingly, the people responsible for the operations. Most organizations use other titles such as production manager, account manager, head teacher, superintendent, floor manager, colonel, or a huge range of alternatives. These are the people with most knowledge of operations – or if they don't have most knowledge they shouldn't be there. They should also be keenest to see improvements. So the first place to start looking for improvements is to ask the operations managers. They will have lots of ideas that they haven't had time to develop, or nobody has asked for their opinion.

In brief

Operations managers are most closely concerned with operations, and they are in the best position to suggest, design and implement improvements.

WAY 36 LOOK FOR IMPROVEMENTS IN DIFFERENT PLACES

There are many places you can look for improvements in operations. The operations strategy defines the overall policies for operations and gives the framework for lower decisions. Medium-term tactical decisions consider the layout of facilities, process design, capacity planning, production planning, make/buy decisions, quality assurance, maintenance plans, recruiting and so on. Short-term operational decisions include resource scheduling, inventory control, reliability and purchasing.

Perhaps I should mention the obvious difficulty with terms here. Operations managers make decisions at all levels, and it is just unfortunate that low-level decisions are called operational decisions. So operations managers make strategic, tactical and operational decisions about operations. Table 4.2 shows some examples of their decisions.

Table 4.2 Operational decisions

Decision type	Typical operations Management decisions
Strategic decisions	
Business	What business are we in?
Product	What products do we make?
Process	How do we make the products?
Location	Where do we make products?
Capacity	How big are the facilities?
Quality management	How good are the products?
Tactical decisions	
Layout	How are the operations arranged?
Organization	What is the best structure?
Product planning	When should we introduce a new product?

Quality assurance	How is planned quality achieved?
Logistics	How should the supply chain be organized?
Maintenance	How should we maintain and replace equipment?
Staffing	Which people do we employ?
Technology	What level is best for planned production?
Make/buy	Is it better to make or buy materials?

Operational decisions

Scheduling	When should we do each task?
Staffing	Who will do the scheduled operations?
Inventory	How do we organize the stocks?
Reliability	How can we improve equipment reliability?
Maintenance	When do we schedule maintenance periods?
Quality control	Are products reaching designed quality?
Job design	What is the best way to do operations?
Work measurement	How long will operations take?

In reality, the differences between strategic, tactical and operational decisions are not this clear. Quality, for example, is a strategic issue when you plan a competitive strategy, tactical when you choose the best ways to measure quality and operational when you test products; inventory is a strategic issue when you decide whether to build a new distribution centre, tactical when you decide how much to invest in stock and operational when you decide how much to order this week.

In brief

You can look for improvements in many areas of operations – don't limit yourself to the obvious ones.

WAY 37   LOOK AT THE OPERATIONS OF OTHER ORGANIZATIONS

There is nothing wrong with learning from other organizations, as we saw with benchmarking in Way 9. When British Airways first started to update their operations in the 1980s, Roger Davies said, 'SAS (Scandinavian Airlines System) was our first cultural benchmark.' But they also looked at other airlines, hotels and any other place they could learn lessons. Xerox started benchmarking by looking at the customer service in L L Bean which says, 'Our products are guaranteed to give 100 per cent satisfaction in every way. Return anything purchased from us at any time if it proves otherwise... we do not want you to have anything from L L Bean that is not completely satisfactory.'

You should search every reasonable source for ideas that you can adapt – don't be afraid or too proud to borrow ideas from anyone. Remember that 'to copy from one person is plagiarism, to copy from lots of people is research'. If you offer a service, you might start by looking at the operations of a highly successful service provider like Tesco. This is the largest supermarket chain in the country, with an annual turnover approaching £20 billion, and an enviable record of customer service. You can learn a lot by walking around a Tesco store. See how they have tackled their decisions about:

- location;
- layout;
- capacity;
- product design;
- process design;
- performance measures;
- logistics;
- stock control;
- technology used;
- staffing;
- pricing;

- amount of vertical integration;
- maintenance and replacement;
- financing.

These decisions in a Tesco supermarket are similar to decisions in every other organization. When LG of Korea decided to invest £1.7 billion in television monitor and microchip plants in Newport, South Wales, it looked at a range of similar decisions – as did Graham Barnet when he started a painting and decorating business in Nottingham.

In brief

When you look for improvements, see how other organizations have solved similar problems, and don't be afraid to borrow good ideas.

WAY 38   MEASURE PRODUCTIVITY

You are likely to be judged – at least to some extent – by your financial performance. But financial measures such as profitability and return on investment are really indirect measures of the operations; good financial performance comes from good operations. You can measure the operations more directly using measures such as productivity, utilization and efficiency.

Productivity is the most common measure of operations. It shows the amount of output that you create for each unit of resource used. You might, for example, measure the number of units made per employee, sales per square metre, or deliveries per vehicle.

Your competitors are always trying to gain an advantage, and an effective way of doing this is by increasing their productivity. You then have to match their improvement simply to stay in business. So the benefits of higher productivity include:

- long-term survival;
- lower costs;
- less waste of resources;
- higher profits, wages, real income, etc;
- targets for continually improving operations;
- comparisons between operations;
- measures of management competence.

These are good reasons for improving productivity. But how can you do it? Harvey Robbins and Michael Finley are misleading when they say, 'It is always possible to boost productivity. At the very worst, you simply make people work harder – problem solved' (1997). In reality there are four ways of increasing productivity:

1. improve effectiveness – with better decisions;
2. improve efficiency – with a process that gives more output for the same inputs;
3. improve the process – getting higher quality, fewer accidents, or less disruption;
4. improve motivation – getting better results from the workforce.

One of the problems with improving productivity is that employees see it as an excuse for sacking them. In 1999 BMW were worried by poor productivity at their Longbridge Rover plant and discussions focused on the loss of 6,000 jobs. In reality, productivity didn't improve by sacking people – but by investing £4 billion in new production lines. The new processes improved productivity, not the staff reduction. At the same time Nissan's Sunderland plant was described by Andrew Lorenz of the *Sunday Times* as 'Europe's most efficient', and they were planning to increase the workforce by 5,000. No one suggested that hiring more people would reduce Nissan's productivity.

Productivity is really a measure of management performance, and it has very little to do with the old-fashioned idea of getting people to work harder. An enthusiastic person digging a hole with a spade can work very hard, and still be far less productive than a lazy person with a bulldozer. Typically, 85 per cent of productivity is set by the process which is designed by managers and only 15 per cent is due to the individual workers.

In brief

Productivity is the most common direct measure of how well you do your operations.

WAY 39   DEFINE PRODUCTIVITY CAREFULLY

When you talk about productivity, you have to be careful to explain exactly what you mean. Airline Food Services introduced a semi-automatic process for preparing meals, and they recorded the figures shown in Table 4.3.

Table 4.3 Meal preparation

	Old system	New system
Meals prepared a day	12,000	18,000
Number of employees	120	100
Asset value	£300,000	£900,000

The operations manager was happy to report that productivity had increased from 100 meals per employee to 180 meals per employee. Unfortunately, the finance manager had to report that productivity had fallen from 40 meals to 20 meals per £1,000 of assets employed.

You can give the illusion of better productivity by changing your definitions – like Mrs Thatcher's government which changed the meaning of 'unemployed' 16 times. This is just dishonest. Total productivity is clearly defined as total output from a process divided by the total input.

$$\text{Total productivity} = \frac{\text{total output}}{\text{total input}}$$

Unfortunately, this measure has several drawbacks, and is seldom used. To start with, the input and output must be in the same units, so they are translated into a common currency. This depends on the accounting conventions used, and you no longer have an objective measure. Another problem is finding the values of all the inputs and outputs. How, for example, do you put a value on fresh water, sunlight, waste products or pollution?

There's an old story about a rowing match between a Japanese company and a British one. The Japanese boat won the race

convincingly, and their eight rowers and cox went away to cele-
brate. The British boat contained a chief executive, three directors,
four senior managers and one rower. The managers were
appalled at the rower's low productivity and sacked him.

In brief

When talking about productivity, you have to explain exactly
what you mean.

WAY 40   USE PARTIAL PRODUCTIVITIES

Total productivity is difficult to use, so you will normally use partial productivity. Partial productivity shows the total output
related to one particular input, such as the amount produced per
person, the output per machine-hour, or the sales per £1 of asset
value.

$$\text{Partial productivity} = \frac{\text{total output}}{\text{amount of one input used}}$$

To make the calculation even easier, the 'total output' only
includes products and does not include secondary outputs like
waste, by-products and scrap. You usually relate partial productivity to four types of resource:

- *equipment productivity*, such as the units made per
  machine-hour, or miles driven per vehicle;
- *labour productivity*, such as the units made per person, or
  tonnes produced per shift;
- *capital productivity*, such as the units made for each £1
  invested, or sales per unit of capital;
- *energy productivity*, such as the units of output per kilowatt-hour of electricity, or units made for each £1 spent on
  energy.

You should always choose measures that give a reliable view of
performance. It would make no sense to judge the productivity of
an automatic telephone exchange by the number of calls per
employee, or the productivity of a bank by the number of transactions per kilowatt-hour of electricity. But any single measure gives

only one, limited view of your organization. To get a broader view you need a cocktail of different measures for different aspects of operations. You could, for example, judge a hospital by the length of its waiting lists, cost of treatment, quality of care, severity of illness, types of patients, treatments used, research work, training and teaching standards, community service and so on. Unfortunately, many of these measures are based on opinions, and it is difficult to get a convincing overall picture. This is particularly true with services like the police, army and fire service, which are most successful if they don't work at all – implying there are no crimes, wars or fires.

In brief

Partial productivity gives useful measures, but you have to choose the measures carefully.

WAY 41   USE OTHER MEASURES OF PERFORMANCE

It is often difficult to measure productivity, especially when the output from a process is unclear. How can you value the output from a nurse, policeman, civil servant or teacher? There is no convincing answer to this, as you could see from the heated debate when Kenneth Clarke was Chancellor of the Exchequer and announced that 'there can be no pay rises for workers in the public sector unless paid for by increases in productivity'.

So the problems with productivity include:

- it has to be carefully defined;
- it may not give a useful measure of overall performance;
- the difficulty of putting a value on all inputs and outputs;
- the difficulty of combining different types of inputs and outputs;
- it cannot includes subjective values like quality;
- some products, like legal services, are unique.

You can use several other measures to get around these problems. A basic measure of performance is capacity, which sets the amount of a product that you can make in a specified time. Production is the amount that you actually make. These two are related through the utilization, which measures the amount of available capacity that you actually use.

Efficiency describes the percentage of possible output that is actually achieved. If people working in an office can process five forms in an hour, but someone has just spent an hour processing four forms, their efficiency is $4/5 = 0.8$ or 80 per cent. Sometimes people confuse efficiency with effectiveness, which measures how well an organization sets and achieves its goals. This is the difference between 'doing the right job' and 'doing the job right'.

Kevin Singh drives a tractor/trailer that can plant 80 acres of bulbs in a 10-hour day. One day he drove the planter for 6 hours and planted 40 acres:

- The capacity is the maximum amount the tractor can plant, which is 80 acres a day, or 8 acres an hour.
- Utilization is the proportion of capacity actually used, which is $40/80 = 0.5$ or 50 per cent. Some people define capacity as the proportion of available time used, which is $6/10 = 0.6$ or 60 per cent.
- Production is the amount actually made, which is 40 acres.
- Productivity is the amount produced in relation to resources used, so one definition gives $40/6 = 6.7$ acres a machine-hour.
- Efficiency shows how well the production achieves the organization's goals.

In brief

There are many other measures for operations and you should use the most appropriate.

WAY 42   AIM FOR ECONOMIES OF SCALE

You get economies of scale when the unit cost falls as the number of units made increases. This is why Volkswagen cars are cheaper than Rolls-Royce cars, and the *Sunday Times* colour supplement is cheaper than a Lesley Hogan limited edition print.

There are three reasons for the lower unit costs:

- fixed costs are spread over a larger number of units;

- you can use more efficient processes, perhaps including more automation;
- more experience with the product raises efficiency.

Economies of scale encourage you to concentrate operations and make as many units as possible in the same facilities. This is why Boeing concentrate their aeroplane production in Seattle, the Driver and Vehicle Licensing Agency works only in Swansea and why village shops are closing down.

Another benefit from larger operations comes from the 'learning curve'. The more often you repeat something, the easier it becomes – which is why musicians and sportsmen spend a lot of time practising. With higher production levels, the time taken for each unit declines.

Obviously, you can't expand facilities for ever, and there is no point in having more capacity than likely demand. More realistically, if you expand beyond a certain size the organization gets too complex – making communications, support functions and management more difficult. Beyond this point you get dis-economies of scale. You can see these in many large organizations, such as governments, which aim for the efficiencies that come from centralization, but actually get bogged down in bureaucracy and red tape.

In brief

Economies of scale can give substantial savings, up to a certain limit.

WAY 43   USE PROJECT MANAGEMENT

Management is usually viewed as a continuous process that lasts without a break for the whole of your organization's life. But some jobs, like building the Channel Tunnel, are clearly projects; they do a specific job, have a distinct beginning and end and a fixed duration. When the job is done, the project is finished.

People have developed special approaches to project management. A project manager often has overall control and can have very wide-ranging responsibilities. The project team does not follow the usual 'line of authority', but is seconded from line functions. This gives a matrix structure where people have divided responsibilities. The control of projects is made easier by dividing them into phases running from conceptual design through to termination. There are also special methods for planning projects, like critical path methods (CPM).

Managers have increasingly realized that they can use these methods in their everyday work. You probably find that a lot of your work is not continuous, but consists of a series of projects. Consultants work for different clients, software houses work on different packages, pharmaceutical companies research a series of new products, marketing departments run a series of promotions.

Project management can bring a lot of advantages to your work. Devenish Howard is a removal company that has developed a simple CPM model for its jobs. It gives the expected times for some key activities, and the computer automatically prints schedules for activities and all resources. More generally, project teams have the benefits of:

- using management methods that recognize the nature of projects;
- solving problems quickly, as the right people are assembled to concentrate on a solution;
- spreading expertise around the organization, as team members move on to new projects and share their experiences;
- using resources efficiently, as they are released to other projects when not needed;
- tightly controlling operations, with constant feedback on progress.

This does not mean, of course, that project management is better than continuous management – as you can see by its awful performance with building the Channel Tunnel and its London rail link, the new British Library, introducing Channel 5, the Millennium Dome and its Underground link, or just about any other major project. But project management does give an additional set of management tools that you might find useful.

In brief

You might get some benefit from using project management tools, particularly if your job is really a series of separate projects.

Focus on Your Products

The purpose of an organization is to supply products that satisfy customer demand. There's almost no limit to the variety of products – but they all need careful planning. As James Garfield said, 'Things don't turn up in this world until somebody turns them up.'

Some companies have made stunningly bad decisions about their products. The classic example comes from Ford, who introduced the Edsel in 1957 – and withdrew it two years later with a loss of US $350 million. But there are many other examples of mistakes. SelectaVision video disc player lost US $580 million for RCA, the Convair jet lost US $425 million for General Dynamics, the PCjr lost US $100 million for IBM.

Even the best plans can go wrong – 'The best laid schemes of mice and men gang aft a-gley' (Robert Burns). But with careful planning you stand the best chance of getting products that customers want, and that make a profit.

WAY 44   PLAN YOUR PRODUCTS

Products can be tangible goods, such as computers, bricks and bottles of wine – or intangible services, such as insurance, education and transport. Most products are a combination of goods and services. At McDonald's the product is a package that includes goods (the food you eat) and fast service; General Motors is the world's largest manufacturer of cars, but its products include warranties and after-sales service.

You have to plan every product so that it contributes to your organization's objectives. If you want a profit, you have to make products that customers buy. Your products somehow have to pass value to customers. As Michael Hammer says, 'The mission of a business is to create value for its customers' (1996).

Product planning is the point where you move from the vague aim of satisfying customer demand, and describe your actual products. This is where you look at the designs and the features that make your products attractive. Unfortunately, customer demand changes over time. In winter we want warm clothing, and then in summer we want clothes that keep us cool; 10 years ago we wanted pine cupboards in the kitchen, but this year we want white ones; we used to want portable telephones, but now we want palmtop communication equipment. Charlie Bell of McDonald's Australia says, 'If there's one constant about customers, it's that they will change – in taste, in attitude and in demands' (Dando-Collins, 1996).

You allow for these changes by constantly checking what customers want, and making sure that you have products to satisfy them. To do this, you keeping asking questions:

- Who are our customers?
- What products do they want?
- How can we best meet these demands?
- What changes do we make to existing products?
- What new products do we introduce?
- How do we make these products?
- What are the marketing and financial effects?

This approach of responding to customer demands was characterized by Jan Carlson of Scandinavian Airline Service who said, 'Our new customer-oriented perspective starts with the market instead of the product. Then the means of production is tailored to give the customer the best possible products' (1989).

In brief

You have to plan products to meet changing customer demands.

WAY 45   DESIGN THE WHOLE PRODUCT PACKAGE

Last year I visited a clothes manufacturer in Poland. The design department looked as you would imagine, full of arty people sketching clothes and experimenting with colours and materials.

Most product designers don't make expensive clothes for a Parisian catwalk, but they are still concerned with every aspect of their product, from the details of the overall package, through to the process used to make it. At Burger King, for example, designers are interested in how their Whopper looks, how it tastes, how customers like it, how to cook it, what the restaurant looks like, the layout of the kitchen, staff uniforms and all the other parts of the product package.

In general, your product is a package that includes:

- goods that customers buy;
- the environment in which customers buy;
- associated items that support the main product;
- items changed, which are customers' goods that change with the product;
- explicit services, which come with the goods and are part of the product specifications;
- implicit services, which are not part of the product specifications, but which customers expect.

When you go into ATS to buy new tyres for your car, the items supplied are the new tyres, the environment is the workshop and waiting area, the associated items are the free coffee and other goods, the item changed is the car which now works better, the explicit service is the guarantee that comes with the tyres and implicit services include the quality of workmanship and worry-free motoring.

If you don't design the whole package carefully, your products won't sell. The best-looking video recorder won't sell if it doesn't have a reasonable warranty, the highest interest rates won't attract investors to a small bank down a back alley and nobody will use a bus service if the vehicles don't look safe.

In brief

You have to design a whole product package with features that customers want.

WAY 46   REMEMBER WHAT MAKES A GOOD DESIGN

A good design needs three features. It must be:

1. *Functional*, so that it does the job it was designed for – it must be 'of merchantable quality and fit for the purpose intended'. This is obvious, but you see many products, from investment services through to bottle openers, that simply don't work. My living-room has what the estate agent described as 'an attractive 1920s feature fireplace'. It's a pity that the room fills with smoke every time I light a fire.
2. *Attractive to customers*. This has something to do with appearance, but includes many other factors (as you can see in Way 47).
3. *Easy to make*. It's no use making a functional product that customers like, if they can't afford to buy it. Your product designs must take into account the process needed to make them – with the best products being fast, easy and cheap to make. Designs that give higher costs, and which you should clearly avoid, have:
   - a lot of work to be done in a long and complicated process;
   - steps that must be done by hand;
   - non-standard procedures, parts or components;
   - too many, or expensive materials;
   - quality of too high a design;
   - opportunities for faults to give low or variable quality;
   - too many variations or different products;
   - interference with the production of other items.

You can increase the efficiency of operations by simplifying and standardizing the product designs. Simplifying means that you remove unnecessary parts so the product is easier to make. This could, for example, mean using moulded plastic parts that snap together rather than metal ones, or using a limited menu in a hamburger restaurant. Standardizing uses common components in a range of different products. This gives easier purchasing, discounts for larger orders, smaller stocks of parts and longer production runs for components.

In brief

Your products should be functional, attractive to customers and easy to make.

WAY 47   DESIGN PRODUCTS THAT CUSTOMERS WANT

There is only one way of finding out what your customers want, and that is to ask them. Use surveys, market analysis, informal talks, focus groups, Web sites and any other way of learning as much as possible about your customers. Then you set about designing products that will satisfy these wants. And you can ignore Oscar Wilde's comment that 'In this world there are only two tragedies. One is not getting what one wants and the other is getting it.'

Of course, all your competitors will be working along the same lines, so you need either a clearer picture of customers' real demands, or a better product. Realistically, you have to design a better product that competes by:

- *Price.* Customers will pay a reasonable amount for a product, usually including a compromise between price and quality. There are, however, some products such as perfume, clothes and luxury cars where it seems better to charge higher prices.
- *Timing.* A television set that you take home will be more successful than a similar one delivered in 10 weeks, and a fast train service between the centres of London and Glasgow will take a lot of traffic from the airlines.
- *Designed quality.* A Wedgwood dinner service has a higher designed quality than paper plates, and the Dorchester Hotel has a higher designed quality than Sunnyview Bed and Breakfast. You don't have to give the highest possible designed quality – only the level that customers want.
- *Reliability.* This is really a measure of achieved quality, as it checks that the product consistently reaches its designed quality. Wales and West Trains might suggest that a journey takes two hours, but if 70 per cent of trains take longer than this, the achieved quality is considerably lower than the designed quality.

- *Flexibility*. Show that you are willing to meet specific customer demands with specially tailored products.
- *Technology*. Sometimes using the latest technology is enough to give a competitive advantage, such as using the latest Intel microprocessor in a computer.
- *Other features*. Many other features could make your product attractive, including service, convenience, usefulness, simplicity, location, colour, designer and a range of other factors.

In brief

Your products' designs must include a range of features that customers find attractive.

WAY 48   REMEMBER THE PRODUCT LIFE CYCLE

Customer demands are constantly changing. There are many reasons for this, ranging from fashions to new regulations. Sometimes there are obvious patterns to demand, such as the increased sales of sun-block cream in the summer, or the peak demand for turkeys at Christmas. Another pattern comes from the product's life cycle. Demand for just about every product follows a life cycle with five stages:

1. *Introduction*. A new product appears and demand is low while people learn about it, try it and see if they like it – for example, palmtop computers and automated checkouts at supermarkets.
2. *Growth*. New customers buy the product and demand rises quickly – for example, telephone banking and mobile phones.
3. *Maturity*. Demand stabilizes when most people know about the product and are buying it in steady numbers – for example, colour television sets and insurance.
4. *Decline*. Sales fall as customers start buying new, alternative products – for example, tobacco and milk deliveries.
5. *Withdrawal*. Demand declines to the point where it is no longer worth making the product – for example, black and white television sets and telegrams.

The length of the life cycle varies quite widely. Each edition of *The Guardian* completes its life cycle in a few hours; clothing fashions last months or even weeks; the life cycle of a washing machine is several years; some basic commodities like Fairy soap and Nescafé have stayed in the mature stage for decades.

Unfortunately, there are no reliable guidelines for the length of a cycle. Some products have an unexpectedly short life and disappear very quickly. Some products, like full cream milk and beer, stayed at the mature stage for years and then started to decline. Even similar products can have different life cycles – with Ford replacing small car models after 12 years and Honda replacing them after seven years. Some products appear to decline and then grow again – such as passenger train services which grew by 7 per cent in 1998 and cinemas where attendances fell from 1.64 billion in 1946 to 54 million in 1984, and then rose to 140 million in 1997.

One thing we can say is that product life cycles are generally getting shorter. Alvin Toffler says, 'Fast-shifting preferences, flowing out of and interacting with high-speed technological change, not only lead to frequent changes in the popularity of products and brands, but also shorten the life-cycle of products' (Toffler, 1970).

In brief

Demand for your product will usually follow a standard life cycle.

WAY 49   MAKE A RANGE OF PRODUCTS

Ideally, you would make a single product – like Henry Ford and his famous comment, 'You can have any coloured car, provided it's black.' This gives the simplest operations, with advantages of:

- making operations routine and well-practised;
- increasing employee experience and reducing training;
- allowing specialized equipment to give high productivity;
- giving long, uninterrupted production runs;
- encouraging long-term improvements to the product and process;
- lowering stocks of parts and finished goods;
- making purchasing and related functions easier.

Unfortunately, customers all seem to want different products, so you compromise by expanding your range. Sometimes this range is narrow, like Northern Dairies which concentrates on three types of milk. Sometimes the range is wide, like Thomas Cook who offer thousands of different holidays. But you should concentrate on one type of product and make variations on a basic idea. British Steel, for example, has the knowledge, skills and experience to make a new kind of steel, but they don't have the expertise to start making perfume. Pearl Assurance introduces new types of policy, Walls sell new flavours of ice-cream and British Airways fly to new destinations. In other words, you look for new products that are similar to those you already make, but are different enough to create new demands.

There are, of course, many conglomerates that make completely different types of products. Virgin has at various times supplied air travel, trains, hotels, holidays, recording studios, radio stations, retail shops, clothing, cinemas, Internet services, personal finance, soft drinks, publishing and condoms. But these companies are usually organized as distinct businesses which act independently.

In brief

To satisfy different customer demand, you should make a range of related products.

WAY 50   INTRODUCE NEW PRODUCTS

The life cycle shows why you should continually withdraw older products and replace them with new ones. When demand declines to an unacceptable level Sony replaces an old model of hi-fi system, the BBC replaces a programme with falling ratings and fashion houses replace their spring collection with an autumn one.

Every time you introduce a new product, you have to do a lot of preparation. This involves six steps:

1. *Generate ideas.* Search for new ideas that you can exploit. These ideas may come from within the organization (research departments, improvements to existing products, brainstorming session, etc) or from outside (customer

requests, competitors' products, new regulations, etc). People often say, 'Build a better mousetrap and the world will beat a path to your door.' Unfortunately, the inventors of thousands of better mousetraps know that this isn't true. New ideas are easy to find; the difficulty is sifting through these ideas, choosing the best and turning them into viable products.

2. *Screen the ideas.* Quickly screen the initial ideas and reject those with obvious flaws. You can reject products that are impossible to make, have been tried before and failed, duplicate an existing product, use expertise that you don't have, would obviously have no market, are too risky and so on.

3. *Technical evaluation.* At this point the initial idea seems feasible, so you add some details to take it from a general concept through to initial designs. Then you can ask: Is the proposed design based on sound principles? Is it safe and legal? Will it work in practice? Can you make it with available technology? Does it fit into current operations?

4. *Commercial evaluation.* This studies the market to see if the product will sell and make a profit. It removes products that customers won't buy, are too similar to existing products, don't fit into existing strategies, won't make enough profit, need too much capital and so on.

5. *Product development.* This leads to the final product design and the process used to make it, incorporating results from previous tests, customer surveys and any other relevant information.

6. *Product launch.* Production starts and the new product is launched. This is the first chance to see whether all the planning and preparation has worked, and customers actually like the product. Only 1 or 2 per cent of the original ideas might come through to the launch stage, and not all of the remaining products will go on to be successful and make a profit.

In brief

You need to develop new products carefully to meet changing customer demands.

WAY 51   USE CONCURRENT DEVELOPMENT

It takes a long time to develop new products. Warner Home Video took more than 10 years to get films on DVDs, Cadbury took five years to develop its Fuse bar, and Western Provident took four years to work out the details of its latest life insurance policy. But there are obvious advantages of being first in the market with a new product. The first arrival gains a substantial price premium, it can get a dominant market position and it sets the standards for later competitors. If you can speed up the development of new products, you have a clear advantage over organizations that react more slowly.

You also have to consider the costs, as longer development time ties up resources and delays the point where you begin to generate an income. Rover initially aimed at making 125,000 of its new R75 in 1999, but when delays reduced this to 25,000, the *Independent on Sunday* reported, 'Rover's future hit by launch delay.' McKinsey has suggested that bringing a product to market six months late can typically reduce profit by 33 per cent.

Concurrent development is a way of reducing the time needed for the six steps described in Way 50. With this, you don't wait until one step is completely finished, but start the following step as soon as possible, and work on several steps in parallel. You don't have to wait until all ideas have been generated before starting the initial screening. You can also run the commercial evaluation more or less in parallel with the technical evaluation.

The more overlap you can get, the shorter is the overall development time – and many organizations have reduced this by 30–70 per cent. Of course, concurrent development is more difficult to manage, and needs a lot more co-ordination, but it can bring major benefits.

In brief

You can speed up the development of new products by using concurrent development.

WAY 52   DESIGN ENTRY AND EXIT STRATEGIES

Astra-Zeneca does fundamental research to develop new drugs; Halifax bank designs new types of account; Microsoft designs completely new software. These companies look for the high profits that come from new products, but they have to bear the cost of research and development. In pharmaceuticals, for example, SmithKline Beecham spend 21 per cent of their sales on R&D, and their Chief Operating Officer Jean-Pierre Garnier says that for success, 'The key is research and development productivity.'

These companies follow a product for its entire life cycle, in the way that Polaroid invented instant cameras and continued to make them through maturity and into the decline stage. But most organizations do not start with basic research to develop entirely new products – neither do they continue making a product through its entire life. They find existing products that fit into their range, and modify these to create their own 'new' product. When O'Connor's Irish pub opened in Liverpool, it didn't offer a new product but adopted a well-tried formula.

So organizations generally start supplying a product that is already some way through its life cycle. The time when they start, and later stop, making a product defines their entry and exit strategy. The best entry and exit strategy depends on your expertise and objectives. Your organization might be:

- *Research driven.* These are good at research, design and development, but they lack the resources and production skills to manage a growing demand. They work in the introduction stage, and leave before the growth stage. ARM take this one step further, and do the research to design high-performance Risc microprocessors, but they have no manufacturing facilities and license their technology to Texas Instruments and NEC.
- *New product exploiters.* These look for research that has commercial potential and then exploit it during the growth stage. They use strong marketing and process design to get the high prices available during growth, and then exit when profit margins begin to fall.
- *Cost reducers.* These design very efficient operations, so they enter the market at the mature stage and produce large quantities efficiently enough to compete with organizations

already in the market. They exit when sales fall too low to maintain high production levels.

In brief

You should look at your skills and experience to design an entry and exit strategy.

Aim for Perfect Quality

When you get a new television set, you plug it in and expect it to work perfectly for many years. But when my parents bought their first television set an electrician delivered it, tested it, mended the obvious faults and listed the parts he needed for the more serious faults. When the parts arrived, the electrician returned and got the television working. Then we gently ran it in for a few weeks, and the electrician returned to sort out any new faults that appeared. Eventually the set was working, and we watched the odd programme – but it was always temperamental and valves burnt out as quickly as light bulbs.

This was in the pioneering days of television, and no one would accept this kind of quality now. Our expectations of every product, not just televisions, have risen tremendously. We expect products to be perfect and won't accept anything less. So the moral is clear. If you don't want faulty products yourself, why would you imagine that your customers will accept something less? In the preparation areas of supermarkets you can often see signs that say, 'If you wouldn't take it home to your family, please don't put it on the shelves.'

WAY 53 AIM FOR HIGH QUALITY

Organizations pay a lot of attention to product quality. Ford say that 'Quality is Job 1'; IBM promise to 'deliver defect-free competitive products and services on time to our customers'; Vauxhall say that 'Quality is a right, not a privilege'; thousands of companies advertise that they are 'ISO 9000 registered', and many have objectives of making 'products of the highest quality'. They emphasize quality for four reasons:

- processes can now make products with guaranteed high quality;
- high quality gives a competitive advantage;
- consumers have got used to high quality products, and won't accept anything less;
- high quality reduces costs.

If you make poor quality products, your customers will simply move to a competitor. Although high quality won't guarantee the success of your products, low quality will certainly guarantee their failure. So survival is one of the benefits of high quality, and others include:

- competitive advantage coming from an enhanced reputation;
- larger market share with less effort in marketing;
- reduced liability for defects;
- less waste and higher productivity;
- lower costs and improved profitability;
- enhanced motivation and morale of employees;
- removal of hassle and irritants for managers.

Most of these are fairly obvious – if you increase the quality of your products, you expect people to switch from competitors. But the idea that higher quality can reduce costs is particularly interesting. This goes against the traditional view that higher quality automatically means higher cost. Gucci are well known for this combination, and say, 'Quality is remembered long after the price is forgotten.'

When you take a broader look at the costs, you can see that some of them really go down with higher quality. If you buy a washing machine with a faulty part, you complain and the manufacturer repairs the machine under its guarantee. The manufacturer could have saved money by finding the fault before the machine left the factory, and it could have saved even more by making a machine that did not have a fault in the first place.

In brief

You get many benefits from making products with consistently high quality.

WAY 54 CONSIDER DIFFERENT ASPECTS OF QUALITY

In its broadest sense, quality is the ability of a product to meet – and preferably exceed – customer expectations. But this still gives a rather vague idea of quality, especially as different customers have widely different expectations. As Philip Crosby says, 'Quality may not be what you think it is' (1979).

The problem is that quality depends on so many factors. You can judge the quality of a television set by how expensive it is, how attractive the cabinet is, its size, how easy it is to operate, the clarity of the picture, the colours, what format it uses, how often it needs repairing, how long it will last, the number of channels it can pick up, how good the sound is, what additional features it has and so on. You have to look at a similar range of features to get a fair view of the quality of almost anything. These features might include:

- its fitness for intended use;
- its performance;
- its reliability and durability;
- its specific features, perhaps for safety or convenience;
- its level of technology;
- its design, appearance and style;
- its uniformity, with little variability;
- conforming to design specifications;
- the perception of high quality by customers;
- the ratio of performance to cost;
- the customer service before, during and after sales.

You can't really judge a product's overall quality by looking at some features and ignoring others. You can't, for example, judge doctors' quality by counting the number of patients they see without considering the treatment they give; neither can you judge a computer by its performance without knowing how long it will last, nor judge a government by its defence policy but ignore its handling of the economy. You have to take a 'cocktail' of factors which, taken together, define high quality.

In brief

You should judge quality by a cocktail of factors that show how well a product satisfies customer demand.

WAY 55   TAKE A CUSTOMER'S VIEW OF QUALITY

When you judge the quality of a bottle of wine you include some measures such as the volume, alcohol content and age, but most of your judgement comes from a subjective view of its taste. Every organization faces this problem of knowing exactly how their customers judge quality. Why, for example, do people perceive a blue car as having higher quality than an identical yellow one?

We saw in Way 47 that you have to find exactly what customers want, and then make the products that satisfy them. This includes quality. So you find exactly how your customers define quality and what features they want, and then you make products that meet their demands. Never be tempted to work the other way around, making products and then seeing who will buy them – because the usual answer is 'no one'.

You have to take the customers' view of quality. As Robert Kriegel and David Brandt say, 'In this business environment, "satisfy the customer" is a sacred cow... managers everywhere are imploring their people to put their customers first' (1996). But this assumes that there are two different views of quality: an *external* view, which is how customers view the product judged by a cocktail of factors; and an *internal* view, which shows how the producer views the product, emphasizing how well it achieves designed specifications.

You really have to play down the internal view and focus on the customers' view. This is difficult. As Charlie Bell of McDonald's Australia says, 'It takes some skill and concentration to actually think like a customer and objectively measure the experience you are being delivered instore' (Dando-Collins, 1996). Or as Burns said a couple of hundred years earlier, 'O wad some power the giftie gie us, to see oursels as others see us!'

Years ago I took a pair of Wrangler cords back to the shop when they showed signs of wear the first time I put them on. The shop said, 'It's the way they're made – they all do that.' I bypassed the

shop and sent the trousers directly back to Wrangler, who immediately sent me a new pair. I wasn't surprised when the shop
closed down shortly afterwards.

In brief

You have to take the customers' view of quality and design products that exceed their demands.

WAY 56   MINIMIZE THE TOTAL COST OF QUALITY

There are four costs of quality management:

- *Prevention costs* are the costs of making sure that defects are
  not introduced to products. They include direct costs for the
  product itself (for better designs and materials, more features, extra service time, etc) and indirect costs for the process (design and control, amount of automation, skill levels
  and training, etc).
- *Appraisal costs* are the costs of making sure the designed quality is actually achieved. These include sampling, inspecting,
  testing and all the other elements of quality control.
- *Internal failure costs*. During the process, some units might
  develop faults, and these are scrapped or repaired. The cost
  of finding faults within the process and fixing them form the
  internal failure costs.
- *External failure costs*. Imagine a product going through the
  entire production process and being delivered to a customer, who then finds a fault. The faulty unit must be
  brought back from the customer and replaced or repaired.
  The cost of this work is part of the external failure cost,
  which is the total cost of making defective products that are
  not detected within the process, but are recognized as faulty
  by customers.

In principle, you can find the total cost of quality by adding these
four separate components. In practice, this is rather difficult as
accounts tend to lose them in other figures. As a rough guide,
quality costs might be as much as 20–30 per cent of sales. This is
surprisingly high because customers won't tolerate low quality,

and because organizations are increasingly responsible for the consequences of defects. Pharmaceutical companies are responsible for side effects of their drugs, insurance companies recompense clients for bad advice on pensions and so on.

Design and appraisal costs generally rise with increasing quality, while internal and external failure costs fall. The external (and to a lesser extent internal) failure costs are so high that you should avoid them – and you do this by making products of very high quality. To be precise, you should aim for products with perfect quality.

In brief

Aim for perfect quality, as this generally minimizes the total cost of quality.

WAY 57   INTRODUCE TOTAL QUALITY MANAGEMENT (TQM)

It's easy to say that you should make products of perfect quality, but how can you actually do this? You might be tempted to use more rigorous inspections – but even the most rigorous testing misses some faults. You have to recognize that 'you can't inspect quality into a product'.

A more radical approach comes with total quality management (TQM). This doesn't use inspections to find defects, but makes sure that no defects are made in the first place. The idea behind TQM is that managing quality is an integral part of every operation.

Suppose you go to a tailor and order a suit. You will only be satisfied if the suit is well designed, if it is well made, if there are no faults in the material used, if the price is reasonable, if the salesperson is helpful and if the shop is pleasant. This means that everyone in the tailor's – from the person who designs the suit to the person who sells it, and from the person who owns the organization to the person who keeps it clean – is directly involved in the quality of their product.

As Lee Iacocca says, 'Everybody in the organization has to believe their livelihood is based on the quality of the product they deliver' (1988). TQM involves the whole organization working together to guarantee, and systematically improve, product quality. Its aim is to make products of perfect quality.

It may seem ambitious to aim for perfect quality – or zero defects – but it is really quite common. You would be very surprised if your Midland Bank or MasterCard statement had a mistake, or if your Big Mac, Gordon's Gin, or bottle of milk tasted strange. There are many organizations that routinely achieve perfect quality (all right, to be pedantic, *virtually* perfect quality) – so why should we be surprised to hear that Ulster Quality Mills are achieving the same standards? The aim of TQM is to bring all organizations up to the highest levels of quality.

In brief

Total quality management involves the whole organization working to make products of perfect quality.

WAY 58   ORGANIZE FOR QUALITY

Traditionally, organizations had a separate quality control function to inspect the work of production departments. As you can imagine, there were inevitable conflicts. But TQM says that everybody in the organization plays a role in quality management, ensuring that no defects are made rather than using inspections to find defects. In effect, production departments take responsibility for their own quality.

You can imagine some of the changes that this brings. Each person working on the process only passes on products with perfect quality. If anyone finds a fault, it means that something has gone wrong, and they stop the process to see what has happened. They find the reason for the fault, and suggest ways of avoiding it in the future. This gives 'quality at source', with 'job enlargement' for each person, who is now responsible for both his or her previous job and an inherent quality management function.

This concentration on perfect quality brings major changes to your organization, some of which are summarized in Table 6.1.

Table 6.1 Change through TQM

Criteria	Traditional attitude	Attitude with TQM
importance	quality is a technical issue	quality is a strategic issue
cost	high quality costs money	high quality saves money
responsibility	quality control department	everyone in the organization
target	meet specifications	continuous improvement
measured by	average quality level	zero defects
emphasis	detecting defects	preventing defects
attitude	inspect quality in	build quality in
defined by	organization	customers

Fundamental changes like this don't just happen; they need:

- empowered employees working towards clear goals;
- continuous improvement of the process;
- open exchange of ideas;
- educated people capable of recognizing, analysing and solving problems;
- people who work for the good of the organization and are appropriately rewarded;
- supportive managers who share information.

In brief

TQM gives each person a role in quality management, and this brings fundamental changes to your organization.

WAY 59 USE TQM IN SERVICES

When Connie Cheung tried to introduce TQM into her advertising agency, there were loud protests. We aren't big enough; we do as well as our competitors; no one here knows anything about TQM; we can't afford it; my last company tried it and failed; let's wait until we're not so busy and so on. But the biggest protests came from those who said that the company provided an intangible, creative service whose quality couldn't be measured.

In practice, TQM is flexible enough to deal with all situations, including services. And many services are clear leaders in quality management – such as fast food restaurants, the post office, building societies, telephone companies, Internet service providers and a whole range of other very high quality services.

Even the most intangible service has some features you can measure (like the percentage of letters that arrive on time, the space between aeroplane seats and the number of mistakes in accounts) and some features that need judgements (like the comfort of seats, the helpfulness of staff and the clarity of instructions). To see how good your overall package is, you clearly have to turn to the customers. You have to collect information by questionnaires, telephone surveys, focus groups, or any other method you can think of. Last month I couldn't rate the service of a restaurant, because the scale on my questionnaire only went from 'satisfactory' through to 'outstanding'. But if you run them properly, questionnaires clearly show how well you are meeting customer expectations, and what areas you need to improve.

In their first full year of privatization, the rail watchdog (the Central Rail Users' Consultative Committee) reported 260,000 trains delayed and 47,000 trains cancelled. The rail operators' performance was described as 'appalling' by the chairman of the committee, 'unacceptable' by the minister of transport and 'a national disgrace' by the deputy prime minister. The following year to 1999 brought even more complaints. In the south-west the complaints office received so many phone calls that it only opened between 1 pm and 5 pm to it give time to deal with its huge backlog. You may not be able to measure every aspect of a service, but you certainly know when you get a bad one. Remember John Major's comment: 'Public service means service to the public, not services the public has to put up with.'

In brief

You can use the ideas of TQM for intangible services, even when you can't measure all the attributes.

WAY 60   INTRODUCE TQM PROPERLY

TQM brings fundamental changes to your organization; it is a major step that needs careful planning. The first step in this planning is usually to form a team to manage the changes. This team should examine every aspect of current operations, find the changes that are needed for TQM and show how to achieve these changes. The team does not implement TQM itself, but it helps the rest of the organization change – it is a planner and facilitator rather than a 'doer'.

In practical terms, you need seven steps to implement TQM:

1. *Get management commitment.* You must convince all the managers that TQM isn't just another fad, but brings a new way of thinking that really improves performance.
2. *Find out what customers want.* This goes beyond simply asking for their opinions, and gets them involved in the process.
3. *Design products with quality in mind.* Aim for products that meet or exceed customer expectations.
4. *Design the process with quality in mind.* Consider quality at every point to give a process that can guarantee high-quality products.
5. *Build teams of empowered employees.* Recognize that employees really are your most valuable asset and make sure they are trained, motivated and able to produce high-quality products.
6. *Keep track of results.* Set quality targets and measure progress towards them, use benchmarks to compare performance with other organizations and look for continuous improvement.
7. *Extend these ideas to suppliers and distributors.*

Introducing TQM can take years of effort and continuous improvement, so it's not surprising that organizations fail along the way.

There are many reasons for these failures, including lack of management commitment, lack of planning, managers who didn't really change their habits, not involving the workforce, getting bogged down in bureaucracy, stopping after unpopular early changes and managers who were satisfied with small improvements.

In brief

Introducing TQM is difficult and needs careful planning.

WAY 61   REMEMBER EDWARDS DEMING

Many people helped develop quality management, and some of the early ones are called the 'quality gurus'. Perhaps the best known are Edwards Deming, Joseph Juran, Philip Crosby, Kaoru Ishikawa and Genichi Taguchi.

Edwards Deming did a lot to publicize TQM, but was concerned that organizations did not get the benefits they expected. To help them on the way, he compiled a list of guidelines called his '14 obligations'.

Deming's 14 obligations

1. Create constancy of purpose towards product quality.
2. Adapt the new philosophy of higher quality, refusing to accept customary levels of defects and errors.
3. Stop depending on mass inspection, but build quality into your product.
4. Don't award business on the basis of price only – reduce the number of suppliers and insist on meaningful measures of quality.
5. Develop programmes for continuous improvement of your products and processes.
6. Train all your employees.
7. Focus supervision on helping employees to do a better job.
8. Drive out fear by encouraging two-way communication.
9. Break down barriers between departments and encourage problem solving through teamwork.
10. Don't use posters and slogans that demand improvements without saying how to achieve them.

11. Eliminate arbitrary quotas and targets that interfere with quality.
12. Remove barriers that stop people having pride in their work.
13. Have programmes for lifelong education, training and self-improvement.
14. Put everyone to work on implementing these 14 points.

Deming's 14 points are not a programme that has a fixed duration, but they give a new way of thinking in your organization. They are certainly not the only possible view, but they do give some useful guidelines.

In brief

Edwards Deming was one of the first quality gurus, who described 14 obligations for TQM.

WAY 62   USE QUALITY CONTROL

The traditional approach of quality control:

- takes a sample of units;
- measures the performance of each unit in the sample;
- sees how many of the sample meet designed specifications;
- passes the product as having acceptable quality if a predetermined number of the sample reach the designed standard;
- takes remedial action if fewer than this predetermined number reach the standard.

This approach raises a number of questions. To start with, you might ask, 'Why do inspections, when quality at source should mean that there are no defects?' TQM doesn't mean that inspections are no longer needed – but their purpose has changed. Instead of finding faults that are known to exist, inspections check that there really are no faults and that everything is working smoothly.

Secondly, you could ask, 'Why take a sample of products rather than test every unit?' It is certainly better to test every unit, but there are many circumstances when you can't do this – when testing would destroy the product, is too expensive, takes too long and so on.

Next, you might ask about the level of performance that is acceptable. This is essentially a management decision. You can't avoid some variation in the output of a process, so you have to define 'acceptable quality' as performing within specified limits and meeting customer expectations. Provided your bar of Cadbury's chocolate weighs between 249.99 g and 250.01 g most people don't mind that it isn't exactly the advertised 250 g. But you should make the variation as small as possible – and TQM looks for continuous reduction in variation.

Then you could ask some detailed questions about the samples. How often should you take samples? How big should the samples be? When should you do the sampling? The answers to these questions come from the well-tried analyses of statistical quality control. A huge amount of work has been done in this area, and there are many quality control packages that automatically design sampling plans.

Many years ago I was looking at the sampling of milk in Yorkshire. The big dairies have virtually no problems with quality, but to look enthusiastic we sent 5 or 6 samples per million population each week to laboratories for analysis – something like 700 samples a year. We had a very hard time explaining to a group of councillors that this really was enough, and why we didn't need to test every pint produced.

In brief

Sampling is still an important part of quality management, to check that products are within acceptable limits.

WAY 63   INSPECT PRODUCTS AT THE RIGHT TIMES

Inspections used to be left until the later stages of the process – often just before the finished products were delivered to customers. As there was more chance of a product being faulty by the end of the process, all defects could be found in one big, final inspection. But the longer a unit is in a process, the more time and money is spent on it – so it makes sense to find faults as early as possible, before any more money is wasted by working on a defective unit. It is better for a baker to find bad eggs when they arrive at the bakery, rather than use the eggs and then scrap the finished cakes.

Your first quality control inspections should come at the beginning of the process, testing materials as they arrive from suppliers – and there is a strong case for inspections within suppliers' own operations. Then you should have inspections all the way through the process to the completion of the final product and its delivery to customers. Some particularly important places for inspections are:

- on raw materials when they arrive;
- at regular intervals during the process;
- before high-cost operations;
- before irreversible operations, like firing pottery;
- before operations that might hide defects, like painting;
- when production is complete;
- before shipping to customers.

This may seem like a lot of inspections, but remember that most of them are done by people working on the process. Quality at source means that the products are not taken away for testing in some remote laboratory, but are checked at each step before being passed on to the next step.

For one of my last New Year's resolutions I bought a rowing machine and found a slip of paper signed by 11 people, each saying that the machine was good when it left their part of the process.

In brief

You should do inspections at regular points in the process.

WAY 64   GET ISO 9000 CERTIFICATION

Organizations that achieve certain quality standards can apply for ISO 9000 certification. This is administered by independent third parties who check your quality management methods. For this you must:

- say what you are going to do about quality – describing procedures, operations and inspections;

- show that you actually do work in this way;
- prove that the work was done properly by doing audits and keeping records.

Some people think that the ISO standards guarantee high product quality – if you see the label, the product must be good. But really, the standard only shows that an organization has a programme of quality management, and that the product quality is consistent and reliable. The quality need not necessarily be good. A manufacturer of metal bearings, for example, will specify the tolerance on the diameter of a bearing; ISO certification means that the bearings will be within this tolerance, but it does not judge whether the tolerance is good enough for any intended use.

There are five separate parts to the ISO 9000 standards:

- ISO 9000 defines quality, gives a series of standards an organization might aim for and guides you through the other parts of the series.
- ISO 9001 is used by companies whose customers expect them to design and make special products – it deals with the whole range of TQM, from initial product design and development, through to procedures for testing final products and services.
- ISO 9002 is used by companies who make standard products – it concentrates on the actual process, and how to document quality.
- ISO 9003 deals with final product inspection and testing procedures.
- ISO 9004 is a guide to overall quality management and related systems, and says what you should do to develop and maintain quality.

ISO 9000 and 9004 are guides for setting up quality management programmes; ISO 9001 and 9002 are the main standards; and ISO 9003 describes some aspects of quality control. These standards are flexible enough to use in almost any organization.

In brief

You can show that you are committed to quality by getting ISO 9000 certification.

Design the Best Process

The process includes all the operations needed to make a product. Michael Hammer describes a process as 'a related group of tasks that together create a result of value to a customer' (1996).

There is an important trend in management towards a holistic view of the process, rather than concentrating on the separate operations that form it. The argument is that improving the separate parts won't necessarily improve the overall performance – to get an overall improvement, you have to take an overall view. This integrated approach has led some people to talk of 'the triumph of the process'.

WAY 65   THINK ABOUT THE PROCESS

Many people don't really think about the process they use. Gunther Priesmann has spent 25 years as a solicitor doing the work for buying and selling houses. He says that, 'The work is usually automatic. There is a sequence of procedures that I go through, and as this has stood the test of time I don't see any need to change.' This is a common view of managers, but you can easily see why process planning is important:

- you want to make products that satisfy customer demand;
- the products must, in some way, be better than competitors';
- the process makes the products;
- to make better products you need a better process.

You can make most products by a number of different processes. If you make tables, you can use craftspeople to build them carefully by hand; you can buy parts and use semi-skilled people to assemble them; you can use automatic equipment on an assembly line;or you can mould complete tables from plastic. Each process gives a product with different characteristics. Process planning designs the best process for delivering any particular product.

It's especially important to design the process for services, as you can't really draw a line between the product and the process used to make it. How, for example, can you separate the service given by a bank, theatre or taxi from the process used to deliver it?

There's a huge variety of processes. It is easy to design a process for baking a cake; but if you want to bake 100 cakes for a garden party you will use a different process; and if you want to bake a million cakes every week, the best process is different again. Unfortunately, many managers don't take their processes seriously, and can hardly describe them in coherent terms.

You can start thinking seriously about your processes by recognizing them and describing the details of each. Make everyone in the organization aware of the processes and their importance. Then you can see how well the processes are working and look for improvements. Your processes are at the heart of your organization, and you really should give them the attention they deserve.

In brief

You should emphasize your processes, which consist of all the operations needed to make your products.

WAY 66   BECOME PROCESS-CENTRED

Your organization is probably divided into separate departments, such as R&D, sales, IT and accounts. These departments don't work independently, but should all co-operate to achieve the organization's goals. To help with this, many organizations have become 'process-centred'.

A process-centred organization removes the internal divisions and focuses everybody's attention on the process of satisfying customer demand. As Michael Hammer says, 'Process centering more than anything else, means that the people – all people – in the company recognize and focus on their processes' (1996). When an order comes to a traditional organization, everyone does their separate part of the process and seems to work in isolation – sales collect orders, manufacturing makes goods, warehousing adjusts the stocks, transport delivers the goods, accounting sends out the invoices. The problem is that no one looks after the whole process, integrates different operations, or even makes sure that customers actually get their products.

In a process-centred organization, everyone has the overriding purpose of contributing to a process that leads to satisfied customers. Everyone works as part of a team, with:

- the single purpose of satisfying customer demand;
- concentration on the whole process of delivering products;
- expansion of traditional roles – with empowered employees making decisions and dealing with all types of customer issues;
- responsibility for all aspects of the process;
- access to all types of information throughout the organization;
- a matrix or cross-functional management structure;
- a team leader who has overall responsibility for the success of the process.

This emphasis on the whole process of satisfying customers has many implications. One is that your organization becomes more flexible to customer needs. Last month I asked a monumental mason to make a name plate for my house. Although he didn't normally do this, he was happy to adjust his standard process and make a one-off product. This is typical of a process-centred organization. Traditional organizations imagine that operations are smoothest when customers are kept at a distance; if customers become involved they try to expedite their order, change designs, demand difficult adjustments to the products, ask for detailed progress reports and generally get in the way. A process-centred organization welcomes customer involvement, forms partnerships, increases satisfaction with products and gains a huge competitive advantage.

In brief

You can become process-centred by concentrating everyone's attention on the whole process of satisfying customers.

WAY 67   CONSIDER DIFFERENT TYPES OF PROCESS

One useful way of classifying processes looks at the frequency at which products change. At one extreme are continuous flows, such as a power station that makes the same product without any changes for 24 hours a day. At the other extreme are projects that make a single, unique product, like building the Millennium Dome. With this approach, there are five types of process:

- *Project*. This makes a single unit, usually tailored to individual customer specifications. The process has a lot of variety, needs flexibility to deal with new situations, uses a skilled workforce and general purpose equipment. Projects usually have very high unit costs, but people find them the most interesting to work with.
  Examples: developing new computer software, designing a house, building a rail tunnel.
- *Job shop*. This makes small numbers of a wide variety of products – like the small engineering works where the name originated. Each product uses a different mix of resources – so there are usually some idle resources, while others form bottlenecks. The result is fairly high unit costs, and difficulties in scheduling and keeping track of work.
  Examples: restaurants, general printers, furniture manufacturers.
- *Batch processing*. This makes larger batches of similar products on the same equipment. Bigger batches give smoother operations and lower set-up costs, but higher inventory costs as goods are kept in stock until needed. Batch processing is useful for medium volumes of products, with less product variety and customizing.
  Examples: clothing manufacturers, buses, bottling plants.
- *Mass production*. This is typical of an assembly line that makes large numbers of a single product, such as computers, cars or washing machines. Mass production processes use specialized equipment to make a standard product, with easy scheduling and control.
  Examples: processing photographs, newspaper printing, consumer electronics.
- *Continuous flow*. These are used for high volumes of a single product such as bulk chemicals, oil and paper. The process is

different to assembly lines as the product emerges as a continuous flow rather than discrete units. Such processes use highly specialized equipment that can work for 24 hours a day with virtually no changes or interruptions.

Examples: petrol refineries, electricity supply, paper mills, police service.

In brief

You can use five types of process which put different demands on resources and management.

WAY 68   CHOOSE THE BEST TYPE OF PROCESS

You have to consider many factors before choosing the type of process that is best for your products:

- *Product design*. To a large extent, the product's design sets the best type of process. When Guliano Marelli designs a high-quality suit, the process must really be a handmade project rather than mass production.
- *Overall demand*. The number of units you make obviously affects your choice of process. Artists paint an individual portrait as a project; photographers use mass production to get large numbers of portraits for advertisements.
- *Changes in demand*. Variable demand clearly needs a more flexible process than a stable demand.
- *Product flexibility*. This allows a process to stop making one product and start making another. Lower volume processes are generally more flexible to changes in both demand and product.
- *Human resources*. Different processes need different skills – and the availability of workforce skills, management skills, training and productivity targets can affect your choice of process.
- *Automation*. Higher volumes generally use more automation.
- *Customer involvement*. Customers play an active part in many processes, particularly services, and your designs must allow for this.
- *Product quality*. The traditional way of getting high quality is to use highly skilled craftsmen making small quantities.

This is still best for some products, but automated processes give the highest quality for a wide range of other products.

- *Finances.* The capital costs of different processes vary widely, so your choice is affected by the finances available, return on investment, running cost, etc.
- *Amount of vertical integration.* Some processes put heavy demands on suppliers, and it could make sense for you to control more of the supply chain.

In brief

Choosing the best type of process for your product is complicated, and depends on many factors.

WAY 69   CHOOSE THE BEST LEVEL OF TECHNOLOGY

There are three levels of technology for a process:

- *Manual*: where people have full control over the process, which needs their constant attention – such as driving a car;
- *Mechanized*: where people do parts of the process, but it can work for some periods without further intervention – such as using a VCR;
- *Automated*: which can work without any human involvement – such as a telephone exchange.

In a manual warehouse, people put things on shelves and later remove them; in a mechanized warehouse people control a variety of machines to move the goods; in an automated warehouse a computer controls all the movements. You would generally use higher levels of automation for higher volumes of output. So a rule of thumb is that projects and job shops have manual processes, batches have mechanized processes and mass production and continuous flows use automation. Of course this is only a guideline. The Bacterion Recording Studio, for example, works on a series of projects, but uses very high technology.

Some people find high levels of technology inherently attractive. As Ed Bluestone said, 'Technology has brought meaning to the lives of many technicians.' Among the benefits of high technology are:

- higher productivity;
- working continuously without tiring;
- giving reliable, high quality;
- being fast and powerful;
- doing many tasks at the same time;
- storing and processing large amounts of information;
- doing dangerous or boring jobs;
- reducing operating costs.

These benefits don't mean that you should immediately replace all your existing processes by high technology alternatives. You have to consider many factors before reaching this decision. Perhaps the most obvious is cost, as automated systems have high capital costs which must be spread over higher production levels. Automation can also reduce the flexibility of a process, and create a barrier between customers and the final product – which is why people using tourist information offices walk past computerized information systems and talk directly to a person behind the desk. But perhaps the major criticism of automated systems is that they ignore the huge variety of skills that people can bring.

Overall, you should take the advice of Renzo Piano, who said, 'Technology is like a bus, if it goes in the direction you want to go, you take it.'

In brief

You have to consider many factors before choosing the best level of technology for your process.

WAY 70   LAY OUT THE PROCESS PROPERLY

When you visit a Safeway supermarket you see that goods are arranged in parallel aisles. A lot of experience and experiment has gone into this layout, which encourages customers to buy more goods. Every other organization has to design the best layout for its operations, whether it is an office for CGU, a new production line for Landrover, a distribution centre for Lidl, or the Welsh Assembly.

Well-laid-out facilities are efficient and allow a smooth flow of work through the process, but a poor layout is inefficient and disrupts operations. You can see the difference in bus stations, where some can handle large numbers of passengers very efficiently and others have long queues, with crowds milling around without making any progress.

You can use five different types of layout:

- *Process layouts* – where all similar operations are grouped together. Hospitals use a process layout and put all emergencies in one ward, surgical patients in another, paediatrics in another and so on.
- *Product layouts* – where all the operations used to make a particular product are grouped together. You can imagine this as an assembly line where all the equipment is lined up in order and each unit passes straight down the line.
- *Hybrid layouts* – which give a combination of process and product layouts. An airport passenger terminal has a process layout with separate ticket purchase area, check-in area, cafeteria and duty-free shops – but there are some product layouts, like customs clearance. Some factories have a process layout, but a certain sequence of operations is repeated so often that a special area – or work cell – is set aside to deal with them on an assembly line. A focused factory extends this idea and moves the repeated operations away to a specialized building.
- *Fixed position layouts* – which have the product staying still and operations all done on the same site. This usually happens when a product is too big or heavy to move around, such as on shipbuilding and construction sites.
- *Specialized layouts* – of which there are many different types, such as warehouses, offices, shops, schools and airports. You need special skills and experience to design good layouts for these operations.

In brief

You have to design the best possible layout for your process.

WAY 71   USE FLEXIBLE AUTOMATION

Mass production and continuous flow processes generally use automation to give efficient, low-cost operations. But the intermittent processes – project, job shop and batch – are less efficient and have higher unit costs. Flexible automation is a way of bringing the efficiencies of automation to intermittent processes.

For manufacturers, flexible automation started with numerically controlled (NC) machines. These developed into computerized numerically controlled (CNC) machines, and then into industrial robots and a variety of other machines that work automatically. People use the term 'computer-aided manufacturing' (CAM) for any process where operations are controlled by a computer.

Flexible manufacturing systems (FMS) extend the automatic control by having a central computer to co-ordinate all operations. So the essential parts of FMS are:

- a central computer to schedule, route, load and control operations;
- a number of machines under the control of the central computer;
- a computer-controlled transport system between machines;
- computer-controlled loading and unloading equipment.

Once FMS are set up and working, they can work with very little human intervention.

In brief

You can use flexible automation to bring the efficiencies of automation to intermittent processes.

WAY 72   USE COMPUTER-ASSISTED DESIGN

Software for helping with product design has been around for years. It stores a library of designs, and then rather than designing a product from scratch, you pull out similar designs and modify them as needed. This is the approach of computer-assisted design (CAD), which:

- stores a library of designs;
- allows quick changes to existing designs;
- enhances basic drawings, showing different views and perspectives, changing scales and so on;

- does calculations about strengths and any other physical features;
- produces all necessary drawings and blueprints;
- estimates costs for products as they are being designed;
- generates bills of material and other production information;
- exchanges information with other computer systems.

There are many programs for CAD, ranging from the very sophisticated to the very basic. (I have just been looking at a version of TotalCAD that came free with *PCPlus* magazine.)

You can use computers to design products with CAD, and then use computers to control the process with CAM, so you can easily integrate the two parts into a single CAD/CAM system. This is the first step towards computer-integrated manufacturing. A fully integrated system would include product design and process control, as well as links with marketing, procurement, maintenance, accounting and logistics.

The next level of integration gives an automated factory. This would take product designs from the initial CAD system, and then computers would do all the following steps up to delivering finished goods. Although no one has yet built an automated factory, there seems little in principle to stop them.

In brief

You can use computers to help design products, and form links with other functions.

WAY 73   AUTOMATED SERVICES

You probably think of automation in terms of robots working on a production line. But in recent years, organizations have put a lot more effort into automating services. You would be very surprised if your bank statements, quotation for motor insurance, or airline ticket were not produced automatically. There are, of course, many personal services – such as those given by dentists, lawyers, hairdressers and taxis – which are one-off projects that would be very difficult to automate. But many services – particularly the routine ones that give a standard product – use high levels of automation. These might automatically process customers (like ChampionChips which record runners' progress in a marathon), materials (like baggage handling equipment in an airport), information (like company loyalty cards), or create new services (like Internet shopping). The following list gives some examples of automated services:

- *Offices*. Computers have transformed the clerical jobs of preparing, storing, analysing, copying and transmitting documents and information.
- *Banks*. All transactions in banks are automated, using a combination of magnetically coded cards, optical character readers and cash machines.
- *Supermarkets*. Supermarkets generally use mechanized systems, but they are exploring automated alternatives, such as self-scanning, computer-readable shopping lists, virtual shopping via the Internet, telephone shopping and automatic delivery systems.
- *Postal system*. Postcodes allow letter sorting to be automated, but the need to send letters is being reduced by computer networks, e-mail and fax machines.
- *Warehousing*. Many warehouses are completely automated, with computers recording all stock movements and controlling the physical handling of goods.
- *Reservation systems*. Airlines started using online reservation systems in the 1960s, and these are now used by buses, trains, theatres, concerts and many other events.

In brief

Personal services can be difficult to automate, but many routine services can use high levels of automation.

WAY 74   ANALYSE YOUR PROCESS

It probably seems obvious that you need a clear description of your processes – or how else do you know what is going on? Unfortunately, as we said in Way 65, most managers simply don't have this sort of description. If you are one of this majority, you should describe the details of your existing process, and then start looking for improvements.

There are several ways of describing the sequence of operations that forms your process and the relationships between them. The most convenient ways are based on process charts that classify each activity as:

- *operation* – where something is actually done;
- *movement* – where products are moved;
- *storage* – where products are put away until they are needed;
- *delay* – where products are held up;
- *inspection* – which tests the quality of the product.

An efficient process will obviously have few delays and movements. When Jacqui Cohen looked at her process for overhauling motor boat engines, she was surprised to find that only 93 of the 327 activities were operations. She redesigned the process to get rid of delays and movements, and reduced the time she spent on each engine by 35 per cent.

The following procedure shows how you can look for improvements in your process. The first three steps describe the current process, and the last three look for improvements:

1. Break down the process into separate operations and list these in their proper sequence.
2. Classify each activity as operation, movement, inspection, delay or storage. Find the time taken and distance moved in each step.
3. Summarize the process by adding the number of each type of operation, the total time for the process, the rate of doing each operation and any other relevant information.
4. Critically analyse each operation. Can you eliminate the activity? How can you improve it? Can you combine operations?
5. Based on this analysis, revise the process to give fewer operations, shorter times, less distance travelled and so on. Make sure that each operation can still meet the demand, and if there are bottlenecks adjust the process to overcome them.
6. Check the new process, prepare the organization for changes, train staff, etc and implement the changes.

In brief

A process chart can describe the details of your existing process, and show where to look for improvements.

WAY 75   RE-ENGINEER YOUR PROCESS

Change is inevitable. You have probably introduced dozens of changes to your operations in the past year. Each of these changes improves (hopefully) your operations and moves the organization forward.

This kind of continuous, incremental improvement is a fundamental part of TQM and most other management philosophies. You build a momentum for change that, over the long term, gives dramatic improvements. Toyota spent over 20 years of continuous improvement getting their just-in-time system working properly.

But there comes a time when these small adjustments are only tinkering, and you really need a more radical redesign. Adjusting a poor order-processing system, for example, still leaves you with a poor system when you really need to throw it out and get an up-to-date replacement. This is where re-engineering comes in. Michael Hammer and James Champy originated the term 're-engineering' and they define it as 'the fundamental rethinking and radical redesign of business processes to achieve dramatic improvements in critical, contemporary measures of performance, such as cost, quality, service, and speed' (1993).

The idea behind re-engineering is that you don't look for improvements in your current operations, but you start with a blank sheet of paper and design a new process from scratch. Don Yarborough of BASF's Seal Sands plant describes his approach as 'You take the work, completely tear it apart, then you introduce technology, empowerment, no demarcation.'

Re-engineering does not add any new ideas, and it says no more than Joseph Juran's 'breakthrough theory' of the 1960s. But it adds the element of new technology. Many organizations introduce technology to their existing processes, but they don't change the process. Re-engineering shows that it is often better to fundamentally redesign the operations. Michael Hammer assures us:

'These extreme measures... succeeded far beyond anyone's expectations. These pioneering companies and the many others who followed them achieved breathtaking improvements in their performance' (1996).

In brief

Re-engineering makes radical changes to your processes, particularly when introducing new technology.

Make Plans for Everything

When you have designed your products, you set about making them. This is where you need some planning. The plans give timetables for all operations and resources, and they show what you should be doing at any time. This control is essential for a process, and you should remember that 'Failing to plan is planning to fail'.

There are two aspects of planning. Firstly, there is the demand for your products, which you usually find by forecasting. Secondly, there are the resources available to make the products. Your plans show how you organize resources to meet the forecast demand.

Like other decisions, you have to plan at different levels from strategic through to operational. The result should be a co-ordinated set of plans which gives the timing for all aspects of your processes. Designing such plans is notoriously difficult.

WAY 76 FORECAST DEMAND FOR PRODUCTS

Your plans show how you are going to organize resources to meet the demand for your products. Unfortunately, the demand for almost every product varies over time, and you don't know exactly what it will be in the future. The best you can do is forecast the likely value. If you forecast properly, and everything works as expected, the forecast should give a reasonable estimate of future demand.

There are many ways of forecasting, but none of them is always the most accurate. You really have to look at a variety of methods and find the best for your specific circumstances. In general, your choice of method depends on factors such as:

- the time covered by the forecast;
- availability and relevance of historical data;

- type of product, particularly the balance between goods and services;
- variability of demand;
- accuracy needed and cost of errors;
- benefits expected from the forecasts;
- amount of money and time available.

Your main decision is whether to use a qualitative forecast or a quantitative one. If you already make a product and have figures of past demand, you can use these in a quantitative forecast. If you are introducing an entirely new product, you have no figures of past demand and must use a qualitative method which relies on subjective views and opinions.

Whichever route you take, it's important that you don't leap into forecasting without enough preparation. You should, at least, think about the following points:

- What is the purpose of the forecast? What are you trying to forecast? Why? How will you use the forecast? When do you need it, and in how much detail?
- What time period should the forecast cover?
- What is the best forecasting method? (See Ways 77 and 78.)
- What historical data do you need? How can you check the data and models?
- How do you set parameters for the forecasts? Or measure the quality of forecasts?
- Will it be difficult to implement the results of the forecast? How can you track the performance of the forecasts? What happens if the errors are too big?

In brief

Plans depend on the future demand for your product, and you generally find this from forecasts.

WAY 77   USE JUDGEMENTAL FORECASTS

Judgemental forecasts are based on subjective views – often the opinions of experts in the field. Suppose a company like Unilever is about to market an entirely new product, or the board of Diageo is looking at plans for 25 years in the future. They won't have any relevant historical data for a quantitative forecast. Sometimes there is a complete absence of data, and at other times the data is unreliable or irrelevant to the future.

Quantitative forecasts are always more reliable, but when you don't have the necessary data, you have to use a judgemental method. There are five widely used methods:

- *Personal insight*. This uses a single person who is familiar with the situation to produce a forecast based on his or her own judgement. This is the most widely used forecasting method – but is unreliable and often gives very bad results.
- *Panel consensus*. This collects together a group of experts to make a forecast. If there is no secrecy and the panel talk freely and openly, you can find a genuine consensus. On the other hand, there may be difficulties in combining the views of different people.
- *Market surveys*. Sometimes even groups of experts don't have enough knowledge to give a reasonable forecast about, for example, the launch of a new product. Then market surveys collect data from a sample of potential customers, analyse their views and make inferences about the population at large.
- *Historical analogy*. If you are introducing a new product, you might have a similar product that you launched recently, and assume that demand for the new product will follow the same pattern. If a publisher is selling a new book, it can forecast the likely demand from the actual demand for a similar book it published earlier.
- *Delphi method*. For this you contact a number of experts by post and give each a questionnaire to complete. Then you analyse the replies from the questionnaires and send summaries back to the experts. You ask them if they would like to reconsider their original reply in the light of the summarized replies from others. This is repeated several times – usually between three and six – until the range of opinions is narrow enough to help with decisions.

In brief

If there is no historical data, you have to use a judgemental forecast.

WAY 78   USE QUANTITATIVE FORECASTS

There are two types of quantitative forecast.

Projective methods look at the pattern of past demand and extend this into the future. If demand for a product over the past four weeks has been 20, 30, 40 and 50 units, a reasonable forecast for demand next week is 60 units. There are dozens of methods of projective forecasting, with the most popular based on moving averages or exponential smoothing.

Causal methods analyse the effects of outside influences and use these to forecast. The sales of a product might be related to the number of salespeople employed. Then you can forecast the likely sales for next year by looking at the size of the planned sales force.

There are many examples of this kind of relationship. Sales of a product depend on the price charged; the number of reports written depend on the number of consultants employed; the output from a machine depends on the speed setting; productivity depends on bonus payments; the amount of money borrowed depends on interest rates; crop size depends on the amount of fertilizer used. In all such examples, you can use the known value for one variable to forecast the value of a second variable. This is the approach used in regression models.

There are many packages (of variable quality) that you can use for quantitative forecasts. But you should not assume that they are based on rigid rules or will inevitably give the right answers. Alvin Toffler said, 'The future is not "knowable" in the sense of exact predictions. Life is filled with surrealistic surprise. Even the seemingly "hardest" models and data are frequently based on "soft" assumptions' (1990).

In brief

When you have historical data, you can use the more reliable quantitative forecasts.

WAY 79   CHOOSE THE BEST METHOD OF FORECASTING

It's often difficult to find the best forecasting method for a specific purpose, as you can guess from the number of forecasts that have gone dramatically wrong. 'Man won't fly in a thousand years' – Wilbur Wright; 'I think there is a world market for about five computers' – Thomas Watson; 'I hold that [California and New Mexico] are not worth a dollar' – Senator Daniel Webster; ' I cannot imagine any condition which could cause this ship to founder' – Captain Smith of the *Titanic*; etc, etc.

There is no way of making an absolutely accurate forecast. Remember that 'all forecasts are wrong – especially when they talk about the future'. In January 1999 the *Sunday Times* asked 11 of 'the city's top strategists' to forecast the level of the FTSE at the end of the year. The forecast went from 5,600 to 6,800 – a range of 20 per cent around the average.

Forecasts are always likely to be wrong because of the random events that you can't foresee. You can minimize the effects of this 'noise' by using a reliable forecasting method, choosing the best parameters, looking at aggregate demand rather than individual demands and making short-term forecasts rather than long-term ones. But you can't eliminate the effects completely. This doesn't mean that forecasts are no use. They are the best figures you can get, and the alternative is to make decisions in complete ignorance. The forecasts allow you to plan, and as Thomas Fuller said in 1732, 'He that fears not the future may enjoy the present.'

A good forecast should obviously have small errors, but it should also:

- forecast things that you really want – and not similar things that are easier to find;
- be ready in time for its intended use;
- be cost-effective;
- use available historical data;
- be in a useful format and easy to understand;
- be accurate, unbiased and give an idea of the range of likely errors;
- be responsive to changing conditions, but not unduly affected by the odd unusual result.

In brief

Even the best forecasts are likely to have some errors, but these should be small if you do the forecasting properly.

WAY 80   TRY TO SMOOTH OPERATIONS

You need plans to organize your resources as efficiently as possible to meet forecast demand. Unfortunately, there is an obvious problem here. Demand for a product varies over time – but the process is most efficient when it works at a constant rate. Smooth production brings many advantages, including:

- planning is easier;
- there are no problems with changes;
- there is no need to 'hire-and-fire' employees;
- employees have regular work patterns;
- larger batch sizes reduce costs;
- stocks can be reduced;
- throughput is faster;
- experience with a product reduces problems.

Your plans have to find the best compromise between a variable demand and steady production. You could simply vary production so that it exactly matches forecast demand. This is sometimes the only alternative, especially with services, but the constantly changing schedules can be very disruptive. Alternatively, you could make products at a constant rate equal to the average forecast demand. This is often used by large-scale manufacturers, but it needs expensive stocks of finished goods.

The usual solution is to find a compromise, where there are some changes in production, but not every period. This gives a smoother output, but with some short-term adjustments. With this approach you have to co-ordinate different levels of planning, so that short-term schedules fit in with the longer-term objectives. A common approach considers the following levels:

- *Capacity plans*, which are the strategic plans that make sure that there is enough capacity to meet the long-term demand;
- *Aggregate plans*, which are tactical plans that show the overall production for families of products, typically by month at each location;
- *Master production schedules*, which are tactical plans that show the detailed timetable of production for each product, typically by week;

- *Short-term schedules*, which are operational plans showing detailed timetables for jobs, equipment, people and other resources, typically by day.

In brief

You need different levels of plans to match available resources to forecast demand, with a target of smooth operations.

WAY 81   APPROACH PLANNING PROPERLY

Your plans have to give schedules for all operations and resources, which are workable, reasonably efficient, keep within constraints – and include a range of complicating factors such as objectives, capacity, timing, cost, quality, demand, details of operations, materials, human resources, marketing and so on. Planning is a complicated job, but there's a standard general approach with the following six steps:

1. Look at forecast demand and find the resources needed.
2. Find the resources currently available.
3. Identify mismatches between the resources needed and those available.
4. Generate alternative plans for overcoming any mismatch.
5. Compare these alternative plans and choose the best.
6. Implement the best plan – then monitor and control its progress.

This approach is sometimes called 'resource requirement planning'.

Unfortunately, taking the steps in this straightforward sequence doesn't usually work. There's a huge number of possible plans you could find in step 4, and you can't described them all, let alone compare the details. A more realistic view of planning replaces the single run through with an iterative approach. For this you design a plan and see how close it gets to achieving your objectives; if the plan performs badly, you modify it and look for improvements. In effect, you repeat steps 4 and 5 in the planning procedure until you get an acceptable result.

Notice that you'll find a reasonable plan that satisfies your needs, rather than some 'optimal' plan which is the best available. This accepts the fact that there is rarely such a thing as a single optimal solution, and if there was you wouldn't be able to find it.

In brief

Planning is usually an iterative procedure to find a reasonable plan that satisfies your requirements.

WAY 82   DESIGN CAPACITY PLANS

The capacity of a process is the maximum amount of a product that it can make in a specified time. If an enquiry desk takes 5 minutes to deal with a customer, it has a capacity of 12 customers an hour. Capacity measures the rate of output, and should always refer to some relevant time period.

Sometimes the capacity of an operation seems obvious – the number of seats in a theatre, or beds in a hospital. At other times the capacity is not so clear. How, for example, can you find the capacity of a supermarket, university or bank? In practice, you find these by discussion and agreement rather than calculation – so the maximum class size in St Hilary's School is an agreed number of pupils rather than a limit set by the building.

Capacity planning starts with your forecast of long-term demand. In principle, all you have to do is build enough capacity to meet this demand. Things are, of course, rarely this simple. It can be expensive to increase capacity by building more facilities or employing more people. So you can use the general procedure described in Way 81 to match available capacity to forecast demand.

Unfortunately, the capacity of a process changes over time, depending on how hard people work, illnesses, the number of interruptions, the quality needed, the efficiency of equipment, pressure exerted by managers, effects of the learning curve and a wide range of other factors. At the same time, different mixes of products use different amounts of resources, so that not all of the available capacity can be used. A product might use all the available supply of one resource, but leave all other resources with spare capacity. The fully-used resource forms a bottleneck, which limits the capacity of the whole process. Jameson Restaurant can cook 200 meals in an evening, but can seat only 100 customers, so the bottleneck which limits capacity is the seating. They can increase capacity only by adding more seats – improving the kitchen has no effect at all on capacity. This seems obvious, but there are countless examples of organizations that don't recognize their real constraints.

I once visited a knitwear factory where sales of jumpers were rather disappointing. They recruited a new marketing manager who built an energetic and enthusiastic marketing team – but without success. Unfortunately, nobody had realised that the newly downsized production department was working at full capacity. To increase sales they had to increase production capacity, not try harder at selling.

There must always be a bottleneck that constrains overall capacity. In the 1970s there was a story about the difference between shops in the USSR and the United States: in the USSR there was nothing to buy but lots of people to serve you; in the United States there was lots to buy but no one to serve you.

In brief

Capacity planning matches the maximum amount of output to the long-term demand.

WAY 83   ALLOW SHORT-TERM ADJUSTMENTS TO CAPACITY

Capacity planning is largely a strategic function – with capacity typically increased by building another facility. But some aspects of capacity planning are shorter term, and you might rent extra space, or work overtime for a spell. So the objective of capacity planning is to make sure that capacity matches forecast demand over the long term, with short-term adjustments to allow for variations.

There are two ways of correcting short-term mismatches between supply and demand. Firstly, *demand management*, which adjusts the demand to match available capacity. Many organizations adjust the demand by simply changing prices – but the prices must be high enough to cover all costs, low enough to be competitive and not change so often that customers are confused. Other ways of adjusting demand include:

- changing the marketing effort;
- offering incentives, such as discounts for off-peak telephone calls;
- changing related products, so they can substitute for products in short supply;
- keeping spare units in stock to be used later;
- varying the lead time, making customers wait for products in short supply;
- using a reservation or appointment system.

One unusual effect of demand management is that organizations may actively discourage customers at times of high demand. This seems strange, but is really quite common. Professional institutions put up barriers against newcomers wanting to join; expensive cars have long delivery times; artists make limited edition prints; and perfumes command very high prices to discourage mass sales.

Secondly, *capacity management* adjusts the capacity to match forecast demand. The obvious way of doing this is to change the working time, using overtime to increase capacity or short time to reduce it. Other ways of adjusting capacity include:

- changing the total hours worked, by changing the number of shifts;
- scheduling work patterns so that the number of people working varies with demand;
- employing part-time staff to cover peak demand;
- using outside contractors, or renting extra space;
- adjusting the process, perhaps making larger batches to reduce set-up times;
- adjusting equipment and processes to work faster or slower;
- rescheduling maintenance periods;
- making the customer do some work, like using automatic cash-dispensing machines in banks or packing their own bags in supermarkets.

In brief

You can make short-term adjustments to capacity, by either demand or capacity management.

WAY 84   DESIGN TACTICAL PLANS

There are two types of tactical plan. *Aggregate plans* describe the production of families of products, typically over the next few months. A knitwear manufacturer, for example, makes different styles, colours and sizes of jumpers and skirts, but the aggregate plan only shows the total monthly production of jumpers and the total production of skirts. The *master production schedule* 'disaggregates' the aggregate plan and shows the number of individual products to be made in, typically, each week. It describes the number of medium red jumpers made in week 1, the number of large blue jumpers made in week 2 and so on.

These two tactical plans answer questions like:

- How many units of each product should you make in each period?
- Should you keep production at a constant level or change it to meet varying demand?
- Should you use subcontractors for peak demands?
- Should you keep changing the size of the workforce?
- Should you change prices?
- Are shortages allowed, perhaps with late delivery?
- Can you smooth demand?

You can use several approaches to design tactical plans:

- *Intuitive approach.* Tactical plans for the next period will usually be similar to those for the last period, so you can use an experienced planner to review the last plans and update them.
- *Graphical methods.* You might find it easier to design plans with graphs, so you might use charts of the supply and demand over time.
- *Expert systems.* These specialized programs use a series of rules to duplicate the thinking of a skilled scheduler.

- *Spreadsheet calculations.* You might find it easiest to compare a number of alternative plans using a spreadsheet.
- *Simulation.* These use computer models of the operations to follow the process for some typical period and report on its performance.
- *Mathematical models.* Formal methods – such as mathematical programming – can give better solutions to some problems, but they are usually limited to smaller, simpler problems.
- *Specialized software.* There is a wide range of software for scheduling, ranging from simple scheduling rules through to complicated enterprise resource planning systems. Most of the suppliers are understandably reluctant to discuss the details of their models.

In brief

Aggregate plans show medium-term production for families of products. Master production schedules 'disaggregate' the aggregate plans to give a timetable for producing each product.

WAY 85   DESIGN SHORT-TERM SCHEDULES

You can use a master production schedule to design timetables for each part of the process. The result is a schedule for every resource, including jobs, equipment, people, material and purchases.

Unfortunately, these scheduling problems are notoriously difficult to solve. The simplest has a set of jobs waiting to be processed on machines (using the terms 'jobs' and 'machines' only for convenience, as you can meet this problem in many different circumstances). You want to arrange the jobs on the machines so that the work is done as efficiently as possible – perhaps minimizing the waiting time, minimizing the total processing time, or achieving some other objective. This seems an easy problem but – along with other types of planning – is notoriously difficult in practice because of the large number of variables. These typically include:

- patterns of job arrivals;
- amount and type of equipment to be used;
- number and skills of operators;

- patterns of work-flow through equipment;
- priority of jobs;
- disruptions caused by customer changes, breakdowns, etc;
- methods of evaluating schedules;
- objectives of the schedulers.

People have put a lot of effort into methods that guarantee good solutions to scheduling problems, but these are generally so complicated that they can't be used for real problems. The most effective way of scheduling is often to use simple rules which give reasonable results. There are hundreds of these rules for different purposes, such as:

- *First-come-first-served* – which is the most common scheduling rule that you see in supermarkets, at roundabouts and in many other operations. It is fair, but has the drawback of delaying urgent jobs behind less important ones.
- *Most urgent job first* – which you can see in emergency departments in hospitals where they treat the patients with the most serious needs first. This gives higher priority to more important jobs, but low priority jobs may get stuck at the end of a very long queue.
- *Shortest job first* – which minimizes the average time spent in the process.

Simple scheduling rules can give good results, but you may need more sophisticated methods. These typically combine a hierarchy of rules with more formal analyses and simulations. A US city was notorious for its scheduling rules for routing snow ploughs – busiest roads first, then roads with steep hills and so on. What made their rules interesting was the recognition that city councillors controlled the snowploughs' budget and complained loudest at uncleared roads. So the first rule for the snowploughs was 'clear the roads between councillors' homes and their offices'.

In brief

You have to design short-term schedules to give detailed timetables for all resources used in the process.

WAY 86 USE OPTIMIZED PRODUCTION TECHNOLOGY (OPT)

One approach to scheduling which has received a lot of attention from manufacturers is 'optimized production technology' (OPT) which is based on the 'theory of constraints' developed by Goldratt (Goldratt and Cox, 1986). Many people have questioned whether this attention is due to the excellence of the method, or the marketing ability of its designers.

The method looks for ways of removing the bottlenecks in a process. When you remove one bottleneck you create another, so it continually looks for ways of improving the current limiting operation. OPT is a proprietary software package and the precise details are not published. But it is based on a series of well-known principles:

- Balance the flow through the process rather than the capacity – so you don't have to keep all resources busy.
- The utilization of operations that are not bottlenecks isn't set by its own capacity, but by some other operation in the process.
- Activating a resource (which means doing work that is really needed) is not the same as using the resource (which might include work that isn't really needed at the particular time).
- An hour lost at a bottleneck can't be recovered, and is an hour lost for the whole process.
- Saving an hour at an operation that is not a bottleneck gives no benefits.
- Bottlenecks control both the throughput of the process and the stocks of work in progress.
- The size of a transfer batch (the number of units moved together between operations) should not equal the size of the process batch (the total number of units made in a production run).
- The size of the process batch should be variable and not fixed.
- Schedules should be designed by looking at constraints simultaneously and not sequentially.
- Lead times are set by the process and can't be predetermined.
- The sum of local optima is not equal to the optimum of the whole.

In brief

You may get better results by using a more complicated approach to scheduling, such as the proprietary software of OPT.

WAY 87   CONTROL THE SCHEDULES

After you have designed your short-term schedules, you have to control the operations to make sure that they actually stick to these schedules. National Express coaches give their drivers schedules for each journey, showing their stops, the number of people to pick up and the exact arrival and departure times. These schedules are well tested and controlled, so the buses usually stick to them closely. On some other services the schedules are not controlled so carefully, and the schedules might be less reliable.

All your schedules need some way of monitoring the operations to:

- make sure the schedules are designed on time, are accurate and kept up to date;
- monitor the jobs to make sure that each is actually done according to the schedules;
- check that materials, equipment, operators and other resources are available when needed;
- check progress as jobs move through the process;
- report discrepancies between plans and actual performance;
- warn of problems with progress, delivery dates or available resources;
- let you adjust the schedules to overcome any problems;
- let you reschedule operations completely if there are major disruptions;
- assign jobs to specific orders and set delivery times;
- give feedback on times, efficiency, productivity, utilization and other measures of performance.

Some control systems are very simple – and you don't have to be a 'control freak' to get good results. You might pass someone in the corridor and ask if they have finished writing a report – if the answer is 'yes' the process is obviously working smoothly. Other control systems can be immensely complicated. Air-traffic controllers, for example, rely on sophisticated communications to control the flow of aeroplanes around airports, and there are many equivalent systems to control the flow of products around processes.

In brief

When the schedules are implemented, you need a control system to monitor progress.

WAY 88   USE JUST-IN-TIME OPERATIONS (JIT)

Just-in-time (JIT) organizes all operations to occur just as they are needed. If materials are needed for production, you don't buy them in advance and keep them in stock, but have them delivered directly to the process just as they are needed. You can imagine this in a car assembly line: just as the chassis moves down the line to a work station, an engine arrives at the same point and is fitted; as the car body arrives at another work station, four doors also arrive and are added. All the way down the line materials arrive just at the time they are needed, and the car is assembled in one smooth process.

As materials arrive just as they are needed, you eliminate stocks of work in progress. But JIT is much more than an inventory control system. It brings a change in the way that you look at operations, often described as 'a way of enforced problem solving'. This grows from its attitude towards stocks:

1. Stocks are held to cover short-term variations and uncertainty in supply and demand.
2. JIT assumes these stocks serve no useful purpose – they only exist because poor co-ordination does not match the supply of materials to the demand.
3. As long as there are stocks, managers won't try to improve their co-ordination.
4. So operations will continue to be poorly managed, with problems simply hidden by the stocks.
5. It would be better to find the underlying causes of such problems, and then take whatever action is needed to overcome them.

This approach makes you think differently about problems. Rather than ignore things that go wrong, JIT forces you to acknowledge problems and find a solution. It avoids one of Murphy's laws which says that 'anything which is left alone will deteriorate from bad to worse'. Parts of the process affected by this thinking include:

- *Quality*. JIT needs materials of perfect quality, so it must include TQM (see Ways 53–64).
- *Suppliers*. JIT relies totally on its suppliers, so it can't allow any kind of friction. It sees customers and suppliers as partners, with the common objective of a mutually beneficial trading arrangement.
- *Reliability*. JIT cannot work if equipment breaks down, so it forces you to solve any problems with reliability.
- *Employees*. JIT recognizes that all employees should be concerned with, and rewarded for, the success of their organization.
- *Responsibilities*. JIT needs people who are flexible enough to do a variety of jobs, adapt to new practices and possess relevant skills and knowledge.
- *Simple operations*. JIT always emphasizes simplicity – by replacing complicated equipment with simpler pieces, moving decisions closer to the work, simplifying product designs and so on.

In brief

Just-in-time organizes operations so that they occur just as they are needed. This gives a way of tackling problems in your organization.

WAY 89   USE KANBANS

JIT aims for simplicity, so it needs a simple way of controlling the process. This is given by 'kanbans' – which is the Japanese for cards.

Kanbans control operations by 'pulling' materials through a process – unlike traditional approaches which 'push' material through. You can see the difference in these approaches by looking at the flow of reports through Westshires Marketing. In their original 'push' system, every stage in the process had its own schedule which was designed to meet the master production schedule. Typically, Jane's schedule said that she had to analyse 10 reports on Monday morning. She took these from her in-tray, and when she was finished she passed them on to Bill's in-tray. Bill's timetable showed that he had to work on the 10 reports on Tuesday morning. Every stage of this process effectively worked in isolation. If Bill had a problem and was delayed, Jane still kept to her schedule and there was a build-up in Bill's in-tray; if Bill finished early he had nothing to do and had to wait until Jane passed him the reports.

Westshires moved to an alternative 'pull' system that links the operations together. This uses kanbans to send messages backwards down the process asking for a delivery of materials. When Bill finishes work on a report he passes it on, and uses a kanban to send a message back to Jane that he is ready to start on the next report. Jane passes this on, so the kanbans pull work through the process.

There are several ways of using kanbans, with the simplest one as follows:

1. All material is stored and moved in standard containers. A container can only be moved when it has a kanban attached to it.
2. When an operation needs more materials, a kanban is put on an empty container and this is taken to the preceding operation. The kanban is then put on a full container, which is returned to the operation.
3. The empty container is a signal for the preceding operation to start work on this material, and it produces just enough to refill the container.

This gives a simple, but deceptively powerful way of controlling a process.

In brief

Kanbans provide a simple way of controlling the flow of materials through a process, by pulling them from one operation to the next.

Manage the Supply Chain

Your organization must have an efficient flow of materials, people and information to support your processes. If you are a manufacturer, you bring in raw materials, information and services – and then deliver finished goods to customers; hospitals move patients, materials and other services; the BBC moves actors, cameras and sets. Logistics is the management function that is responsible for these movements.

The final product of one organization becomes the raw material of another, so your process forms one part of the complete supply chain. The Institute of Logistics recognizes this by defining logistics as 'the time-related positioning of resources or the strategic management of the total supply chain'. They also emphasize the focus on customers by saying, 'The supply chain is a sequence of events intended to satisfy a customer.' In common with most interest groups, the Institute likes to emphasize its strategic role, but in reality it involves a whole range of decisions that are vital to the success of your organization.

WAY 90   LOOK AT YOUR LOGISTICS

Logistics is responsible for the movement of all goods, materials, people and information in your organization. You could use this definition to take a very broad view and say that all operations depend on the movement of resources, so logistics is concerned with everything from production planning through to information technology. Realistically, we have to take a more limited view, like James Cooper who says, 'Logistics is the strategic management of movement, storage and information relating to materials, parts and finished goods in supply chains, through the

stages of procurement, work-in-progress and final distribution'
(1994). This suggests that the key functions of logistics include:

- *procurement or purchasing* – which is responsible for acquiring raw materials;
- *traffic and transport* – moving the raw materials into your organization;
- *receiving* – unloading delivery vehicles, inspecting goods, updating inventory records, etc;
- *warehousing or stores* – storage of materials until needed;
- *inventory control* – administering the replenishment of stocks;
- *material handling* – moving the materials as needed during the process;
- *shipping* – taking finished products, checking them and preparing for delivery;
- *distribution* – arranging transport and delivering finished products to customers;
- *location* – deciding how many facilities to build, and where they should be;
- *communication* – managing information flows and keeping all records for logistics.

These functions – however they are organized – are important for every organization because they:

- are essential;
- are expensive and directly affect profitability;
- provide the main link between an organization, its customers and suppliers;
- affect lead time and service levels;
- can give a competitive advantage;
- give public exposure with trucks and other facilities;
- can be risky, with safety considerations;
- help determine the overall shape of an organization;
- may prohibit some operations – such as moving excessive loads;
- can encourage the development of other organizations.

Unfortunately, logistics is so well integrated with other functions that organizations have only recently realized how expensive it is, and are putting more thought into its management.

In brief

Logistics is an essential part of every process, and it needs careful planning.

WAY 91   INTEGRATE YOUR SUPPLY CHAIN

Logistics is responsible for the flow of all materials through your organization, but it is probably split into several parts. Typically 'purchasing' organizes the acquisition of materials, 'materials management' physically moves them into the organization, 'warehousing' looks after the stocks of materials, 'distribution' moves finished goods out to customers and so on.

Dividing logistics like this creates artificial boundaries that disrupt the smooth flow. Each part looks after its own part of the flow, but nobody sees the overall picture. Purchasing might reduce costs by placing large orders to get the quantity discounts – but the higher stock levels increase the costs of warehousing. Warehousing might look for economies of scale by centralizing stocks, but this increases the cost of transport. The way of overcoming such short-sighted decisions is to have one integrated logistics function.

Integrated logistics moves resources into, through and out of an organization as effectively and efficiently as possible. You have probably heard people describing this as 'getting the right quantity, of the right materials, to the right place, at the right time, from the right source, with the right quality, at the right price'. To be a little more specific, logistics aims to:

- design an effective and efficient supply chain;
- find the best locations and capacities for facilities;
- formulate strategies for the movement of all resources needed to satisfy customer demands;
- manage an efficient flow of materials into, through and out of the process;
- procure appropriate materials from reliable suppliers;

- organize efficient handling of work in progress;
- find the best means of delivering to customers;
- get low costs for storage and high stock turnover;
- maintain good relations with suppliers, customers and other interested parties;
- handle related information accurately and efficiently.

In brief

Logistics is most efficient when it is all organized as a single integrated function.

WAY 92 USE EFFICIENT CUSTOMER RESPONSE (ECR)

In Way 89 we saw how kanbans 'pull' materials through a process, so that everything arrives just-in-time. Efficient customer response (ECR) extends this idea to the whole supply chain. In a traditional supply chain, retailers periodically examine their stock and send orders back to wholesalers. But with ECR – which is sometimes called 'quick response', 'time compression' or 'lean production' – retailers' computers are directly linked to wholesalers. When a customer buys something – say, a pair of jeans – from the retailer, the wholesaler automatically gets a message and sends a replacement.

Once you start this pull of materials through the supply chain, you can keep going backwards. By linking wholesalers' computers to manufacturers, you can send a message back that it is time to make another pair of jeans. Then you can link to suppliers to send the materials needed for the jeans and so on. The result is an integrated supply chain, where a customer purchase sends a message right back to original sources.

The approach of ECR combines several trends, including just-in-time operations, partnerships between customers and suppliers, re-engineering, use of technology, focus on customers and integration of the supply chain. ECR brings the benefits of JIT to the whole supply chain. In a traditional 'push' supply chain, goods spend at least 95 per cent of their time in activities that add no value – like sitting in a warehouse waiting for an order to arrive. ECR aims to eliminate these wasted activities and concentrate on the 5 per cent of operations that add value. Its main benefits include:

- shorter lead times;
- linking supply directly to demand;
- fewer changes of orders;
- fewer mistakes in orders – when, say, demand differs from forecasts;
- lower stocks in the supply chain;
- shorter cycle times and increased productivity;
- faster cash flow.

In brief

Efficient customer response introduces the ideas of just-in-time to the supply chain.

WAY 93 THINK ABOUT LOCATION

Lord Sieff of Marks and Spencer is reputed to have said, 'The three most important things for a successful business are location, location and location.' A nightclub won't succeed in an area where most people are retired; if your major markets are in Western Europe you would be unwise to build facilities outside the European Union; art galleries attract most visitors in the centre of major cities.

Decisions about locations can affect your organization for many years. If you open an office in the wrong place, you might find that the workforce is unskilled, productivity is low, the quality of products is variable and costs are surprisingly high. But once you open, it is very difficult to close it down and move. Rootes were tempted to build cars outside Glasgow in the 1950s, but the factory was in the wrong place and was never a success. Despite spending a fortune to keep it going, it was eventually taken over by Chrysler, then Peugeot, and then closed down.

You might look at new locations because the lease on your existing premises has ended, you are expanding into new geographical areas, your customers or suppliers have moved, there are major changes in your operations, the transport network has changed and so on. But there are alternatives to finding new locations. If, for example, you want to sell goods in a new market, you can do this in five ways:

- *Licensing/franchising*: in return for a share of the profits, you let local companies make and distribute your products.
- *Exporting*: you make the product in your existing facilities and sell it to a distributor in the new market.
- *Local warehousing and sales*: you make the product in your existing facilities, and set up a distribution network in the new market.
- *Local assembly/finishing*: you make most of the product in existing facilities, but open limited facilities in the new market to finish the product.
- *Full local production*: you open complete facilities in the new market.

Local facilities can give greater control over products, higher profits, avoidance of import tariffs and quotas, easier transportation, reduced costs and closer links with local customers. But you have to balance these against the more complex and uncertain operations.

In brief

Location decisions have a long-term effect on the success of your organization.

WAY 94 WORK IN THE BEST GEOGRAPHICAL REGION

When you are looking for new facilities, you have to make a series of decisions about the location. These start with a broad view, looking at the attractions of different countries or geographical regions. Then you consider the best areas within this region, then alternative cities within the region and then different sites within the preferred cities.

Starting at the top of this list, you have to decide which region or country to work in. Typically, you open new facilities in a country where the long-term forecasts show continuing demand for a product – or you open facilities in countries that have lower operating costs. Many companies have opened factories in Asia, South

America and Eastern Europe to take advantage of low wage rates. But if you work in places that are a long way from your customers, you obviously have higher transport costs – and you find that low wages are often combined with low productivity. Labour costs form a very small part of the total cost of many products, so low wages alone don't guarantee low costs.

When you choose the best country to work in, you should consider many factors, including:

- *your organization*: structure, flexibility, experience with international operations;
- *customers*: the number, location and likely demands;
- *existing operations*: how new operations would fit in with existing operations;
- *suppliers*: how materials would be moved to and from the new location;
- *locations of other organizations*: competitors, associated goods and services;
- *infrastructure*: availability, quality and cost of transport, services, etc;
- *costs*: operating costs, wages, transport costs, energy, taxes, hidden costs;
- *economic climate*: currency exchange rates and regulations, development grants, inflation, rate of growth, productivity;
- *social climate*: language, culture, availability and skills of workforce, attitude towards your organization;
- *political climate*: stability, international relations, legal system.

The world is a big place and if you want to expand dramatically you have to go out and find markets wherever you can. As Dryden suggested, 'Look around the habitable world', rather than retire like Shakespeare's Coriolanus whose 'nature is too noble for the world'.

In brief

A series of decisions about the best location for your facilities starts by finding the best country or geographical regions.

WAY 95   CHOOSE THE BEST SITE AVAILABLE

When you have chosen the best country or geographical region, you have to make detailed decisions about areas, towns, cities and individual sites. Ideally you would find a site that is near to both your suppliers and customers. Unfortunately, this is rarely possible, as suppliers aim for the economies of scale that come from centralization, while customers are dispersed over a large area. As you can't find a location that is close to both, you have to compromise. Depending on your type of organization, this might take you nearer to customers (if you run a shop, bank or some other service), or nearer to suppliers (if you run a factory or manufacturing plant).

If you really don't know how to choose a location, you could always copy other organizations. Find where successful competitors work and open up nearby. This is why banks cluster together in one area, car salesrooms in another, art galleries in another and so on. Sadly, this won't always work, as there is contradictory advice. Don't open where the competition is too strong, but look for areas where no one is supplying equivalent products. The choice depends on your operations and aims.

To be more positive, you can use two approaches for finding the best site: firstly, the *infinite set approach* – which looks at the geographical layout of customers and suppliers and finds where the best site would be if there were no restrictions on availability. These models typically look for the 'centre of gravity' of demand. Secondly, the *feasible set approach* – which compares a number of sites that are actually available. The two most common ways of doing this use: 1) *costing alternatives*, to find the total costs of operating in each site; and 2) *scoring models*, which list the factors that are most important to you, and give each a score, with the best site having the highest overall score.

You can combine these different approaches into an overall procedure for finding the best location, which has the following steps:

1. Define the region that you want to work in.
2. Within this region, use an infinite set approach to find a theoretical location for your facilities.

3. Search near this theoretical location to find the locations that are actually available.
4. Use a feasible set approach to compare these alternatives.
5. Discuss all available information and come to a final decision.

In brief

You can use several methods of finding the best site for your facilities.

WAY 96   CONTROL STOCK LEVELS

Stocks are the supplies of goods and materials that you hold in store until they are needed. As there is inevitably some mismatch between supply and use (even in JIT systems), all organizations hold stocks of some kind. A filling station holds petrol until it sells it to customers; a restaurant keeps vegetables until they are prepared for a meal; you stock cash in your pocket until you spend it.

These stocks can be very expensive. In 1998 Zeneca had a turnover of £5.2 billion, an operating profit of £1.1 billion and stocks worth £728 million. It costs around 20 per cent of value to hold stocks (to cover warehouse operations, tied-up capital, deterioration, insurance, etc) so Zeneca might be paying over £150 million a year simply to keep stocks until they are needed. But they have to do this to:

- act as a buffer between different operations;
- allow for demands that are larger than expected, or at unexpected times;
- allow for deliveries that are delayed or too small;
- take advantage of price discounts on large orders;
- buy items when the price is low and expected to rise;
- buy items that are going out of production or are difficult to find;
- make full loads and reduce transport costs;
- give cover for emergencies.

Inventory control minimizes the overall costs of stock by answering three basic questions:

- *What items should you keep in stock?* You shouldn't keep any item in stock unless the benefits are greater than the costs.
- *How much of each item should you order?* If you place large, infrequent orders, the average stock level is high but the costs of placing and administering orders are low. With small, frequent orders the average stock level is low but the costs of placing and administering orders are high.
- *When should you place an order?* This depends on the inventory control system used, type of demand, value of the item, lead time between placing an order and receiving it into stock, supplier reliability and a number of other factors.

In brief

Holding stock is expensive and you should use policies that minimize the associated costs.

WAY 97   USE INVENTORY CONTROL MODELS

You might think that minimizing inventory costs is the same as minimizing stocks. But this is not true. If Wyvale Garden Centre holds no stock at all, it certainly has no inventory costs, but it also has no sales. In practice, there are four costs associated with stocks, and the aim is to minimize the sum of these four:

- *Unit cost*: the price the supplier charges you for one unit of the item;
- *Reorder cost*: the cost of placing a repeat order for an item;
- *Holding cost*: the cost of holding one unit of an item in stock for a unit period of time – such as the cost of holding a spare engine in stock for a year;
- *Shortage cost*: this occurs when an item is needed but it can't be supplied from stock. In the simplest case a retailer may lose direct profit from a sale, but the effects of shortages are usually much more widespread.

The holding cost rises with the amount of stock held, while the shortage cost falls. The aim of inventory control is to balance the competing costs and find policies that give the lowest overall costs. A standard analysis for this finds an 'economic order quantity', which is the best size for a constant order size. This also gives a reorder level, which is the best time to place an order. So you might find that the best policy for a central heating plant is to order the economic order quantity of 25,000 litres of oil whenever the amount in the tank falls to the reorder level of 2,500 litres. A huge amount of work has been done on inventory control systems, and you can find standard results for most common problems.

In brief

There are many models which will help you minimize the total cost of holding stocks.

WAY 98   USE MATERIAL REQUIREMENTS PLANNING (MRP)

Sometimes you can find the materials you need from the master production schedule (see Way 84). If you make bicycles and your master production schedule says that you will assemble 100 bicycles next week, it's easy to see that you need 200 wheels and 100 saddles at the beginning of the week. You can extend this thinking by considering the components you need to make wheels, and finding exactly when you need spokes, rims and hubs. Then you can see when you need the materials to make the rims and so on. This is the basis of material requirements planning (MRP).

MRP 'explodes' the master production schedule to find the demand for all materials, and it schedules these to arrive when they are needed. By matching the supply of materials directly to the demand, it reduces stock levels. It also brings other benefits, such as:

- higher stock turnover;
- better customer service – with no delays from shortages of materials;
- more reliable and faster delivery times;
- higher utilization of facilities – as materials are always available when needed;
- less time spent on expediting emergency orders;
- encourages better planning;
- MRP schedules can be used for short-term planning;
- shows the priority of operations supplying materials.

Unfortunately, MRP also has disadvantages. The most obvious is the huge amount of information that it needs about production schedules, bill of materials, current stocks, orders outstanding, lead times and other information about suppliers. This, together with the amount of data manipulation, means that you can only use MRP when all related systems are computerized and integrated. Other disadvantages of MRP include:

- the systems can be very complex;
- it reduces flexibility as there are only materials for the specified production plans;
- it assumes that lead times are constant and independent of the quantities ordered;
- materials are actually made in a different order to that specified in the bill of materials;
- using MRP to schedule the production of parts can give poor schedules;
- it may not recognize capacity and other constraints;
- it can be expensive and time-consuming to implement.

In brief

Material requirements planning schedules the supply of materials by exploding the master production schedule.

WAY 99   USE AN EXTENSION TO MRP

When MRP became feasible in the 1970s with the arrival of cheap computing, the first users were manufacturers. But services quickly saw that they could use the same approach to schedule their resources. Now hospitals use MRP to schedule surgical operations and make sure that supplies and equipment are ready when needed; restaurants use it to schedule food and equipment; universities use it to schedule teachers, classrooms and laboratories.

MRP has proved so successful that the basic approach has been extended in several ways. The first extensions added feedback. Then if proposed plans would break some constraints, the MRP system detected this and allowed early rescheduling.

The next major extension to MRP is manufacturing resource planning, or MRP II. This extends the range of operations that are scheduled by exploding the master production schedule. As well as materials, the master production schedule can show the amount of equipment needed in each period, as well as the number of people and other resources. You can also find the amount of logistics support, marketing and finance needed. Eventually you can use the master production schedule for planning most of the resources used in a process. This is the aim of MRP II.

In practice, MRP II is very difficult to implement in full. This has lead many organizations to work with partial MRP II, which links together parts of the process and gives schedules for some resources. This, and the fact that MRP II refers specifically to manufacturing, has lead some people to call their integrated systems 'enterprise resource planning'.

In brief

There are several extensions to MRP which you can use to schedule most of the operations in a process.

WAY 100   IMPROVE PROCUREMENT

Procurement is the first stage of logistics – it starts the flow of materials into your organization. Purchasing generally refers to the actual buying of materials, while procurement has a broader meaning and can include purchasing, contracting, expediting, materials handling, transport, warehousing and receiving goods from suppliers. Its aim is to ensure that all the resources needed by your organization are available at the right time. Some more specific objectives are to:

- work closely with user departments and understand their needs;
- buy the resources needed by operations;
- make sure these have reliably high quality;
- make sure they arrive at the right time;
- expedite deliveries when necessary;
- find reliable suppliers, work closely with them and develop good relations;
- negotiate low prices from suppliers;
- keep informed about price increases, scarcities and other problems;

- keep inventory levels low, by buying standard materials, etc.

If you have problems with procurement, these will appear as poor quality materials, late deliveries, wrong quantities, interrupted operations, high costs and poor customer service. Another important point is that organizations typically spend 60 per cent of their income on purchases, and a modest reduction has a significant impact on profits. Suppose that you have a profit margin of 10 per cent. Then a 1 per cent reduction in the cost of purchased goods can increase your profits by 6 per cent. You can check this in Table 9.1, which gives figures for £100 of sales.

Table 9.1 Procurement costs

	Original	Improved	
Sales	£100	£100	
Cost of purchases	£60	£59.40	– reduced by 1%
Other costs	£30	£30	
Profit	£10	£10.60	– increased by 6%

There has been a major change in the role of procurement in recent years. It used to be little more than a clerical job, buying materials as they were requested. Now its importance is more widely recognized, and it has become a profession, with managers expected to take an active part in planning. General Motors spends over US $50 billion a year in purchasing materials, so it is not surprising that very senior managers are involved

In brief

Procurement is the first step of your supply chain, and it makes sure that all materials are available when needed.

WAY 101   IMPROVE DISTRIBUTION

Physical distribution moves finished products out of your organizations and on to customers. If you are moving goods, your distribution might be based around different levels of logistics centres, distribution centres and local warehouses. These distribution systems give a bridge between manufacturers and retailers. They bring several advantages, including:

- manufacturers can get economies of scale;
- factories do not keep large stocks of finished goods;
- wholesalers keep stocks from many suppliers, allowing retailers a choice of goods;
- wholesalers are near to retailers and have short lead times;
- wholesalers can place large orders and reduce unit prices;
- retailers can carry less stock as wholesalers offer reliable delivery times;
- distribution costs are reduced by moving large orders from production facilities to wholesalers.

This general pattern of distribution is also used by services. Airlines, for example, use major hub airports with feeder services to regional airports and then short hauls to local airports; banks collect cheques in central clearing houses before sending them back to branches and customers.

Whatever your product, you have to design the best way of delivering it to customers. Dairies may use fewer staff to carry the daily pint to your doorstep, but they still need an efficient distribution system to get milk from cows to fridges. As Donald Trump says, 'You can create excitement, you can do wonderful promotion and get all kinds of press, and you can throw in a little hyperbole. But if you don't deliver the goods, people will eventually catch on' (1988).

The important thing about distribution is that it makes the final link with your customers. You can make the greatest products in the world, but if they are delivered 10 minutes after a deadline you're not going to be popular. So you have to plan the distribution properly. Start by looking at the number, size and location of warehouses. Then think about the choice of transport – whether it is best to use road, rail, air, water or pipeline. When you have made the strategic decisions, it is time for lower-level decisions about the vehicle fleet, routes, amount of warehouse space, number of people, etc. Remember that distribution is not just another expense that you can't avoid – it is another chance to impress your customers.

In brief

Physical distribution moves products from your process and out to customers.

References

Allen, W (1983) *Without Feathers*, Ballantine Books, New York

Blanchard, K and Johnson, S (1983) *The One Minute Manager*, HarperCollins, London

Bluestone, E (1973) *Maxims: The national lampoon dictionary of humour*

Browne, J (1998) BP boss drives change through the pipeline, Andrew Lorenz, *Sunday Times*, 26 April

Carlson, J (1989) *Moments of Truth*, Harper & Row, New York

Cohen, J, In conversation

Cooper, J (1994) *Logistics and Distribution Planning*, Kogan Page, London

Crosby, P (1979) *Quality is Free*, Mentor, New York

Cushway, B (1994) *Human Resource Management*, Kogan Page, London

Dando-Collins, S (1996) *The Customer Care Revolution*, Pitman, Melbourne

Davies, R (1996) Talk at The Marketing Council, London

Dryden, J (1681) Juvenal, *Satire X*

Egan, J (1996) Talk at The Marketing Council, London

Enrico, R (1997) Shake-up to put sparkle into Pepsi, Garth Alexander, *Sunday Times*, 26 January

Ernst and Young (1992) *The Manager's Handbook*, Warner, London

Farmer, T, Guarantees given with Kwik-Fit products

Fuller, T (1732) *Gnomologia*

Garnier, J-P (1998) SmithKline chief says R&D is the key to the future, Daniel Green, *Financial Times*, 17 April

Gates, B (1994) *Entrepreneur*, January

Goldratt, E and Cox, J (1986) *The Goal*, North River Press, New York

Gooderham, G (1998) Debunking the myths of strategic planning, *CMA Magazine*, pp 24–26, May

Hammer, M (1996) *Beyond Reengineering*, HarperCollins, London

Hammer, M and Champy, J (1993) *Reengineering the Corporation*, HarperCollins, New York

Harvey-Jones, J (1993) *Managing To Survive*, Heinemann, London

Harvey-Jones, J (1994) *All Together Now*, Heinemann, London

Heller, R (1982) *The Business of Success*, Sidgwick & Jackson, London

Iacocca, L (1988) *Talking Straight*, Bantam, New York

Institute of Logistics, Corby, Promotional material

Kennedy, J F (1963) Speech in Frankfurt, West Germany, 25 June

Kriegel, R and Brandt, D (1996) *Sacred Cows Make the Best Burgers*, Warner, New York

Locke, J (1693) *Some Thoughts Concerning Education*

Lorenz, A (1999) Nissan eyes government aid for Sunderland plant, *Sunday Times*, 10 January

McCormack, M H (1995) *McCormack on Management*, Century, London

Major, J (1997) Trust my instincts, *Weekly Telegraph*, 8 January

Mandela, N (1990) Interview in *Life*, April

Marshall, C (1996) Talk at The Marketing Council, London

O'Connor, M (1996) *Qantas Club*, October

Parkinson, C N (1957) *Parkinson's law*, Houghton Mifflin, Boston

Penwarden, G (1998) A balanced approach to providing quality, satisfaction and efficiency, *CMA Magazine*, p 6, April

Perry, M (1996) Talk at The Marketing Council, London

Peter, L and Hull, R (1969) *The Peter Principle*, Bantam Books, London

Piano, R (1996) The 7.30 report, *ABC-TV Australia*, 12 December

Ponting, C (1986) *Whitehall: Tragedy and farce*, Hamish Hamilton, London

Porter, M (1985) *Competitive Advantage*, Collier Macmillan, London

Priesmann, G, In conversation

Robbins, A (1991) *Awaken the Giant Within*, Simon & Schuster, New York

Robbins, H and Finley, M (1997) *Why Change Doesn't Work*, Orion, London

Shakespeare, W (1608) Act III, scene I, *Coriolanus*

Sharman, P (1998) Linking strategy to action, *CMA Magazine*, pp 26–29, January

Sheppard, A (1992) Foreword, in *Developing Your Career in Management*, J G Thorne, Mercury, London

Toffler, A (1970) *Future Shock*, Bodley Head, London

Toffler, A (1985) *The Adaptive Corporation*, Gower, Aldershot

Toffler, A (1990) *Powershift*, Bantam, New York

Treacy, M and Weirsema, F (1995) *The Discipline of Market Leaders*, Addison-Wesley, Reading

Trump, D (1988) *The Art of the Deal*, Century Hutchinson, London

Waitley, D (1995) *Empires of the Mind*, Nicholas Brealey, London

Wild, R (1995) *Production And Operations Management*, Cassell, London

Wilde, O (1890) *The Critic as Artist*

Yarborough, D (1999) Teeside plant seeks to engineer a more certain future, Chris Tighe, *Financial Times*, 8 February

Index

Visit Kogan Page on-line

Comprehensive information on
Kogan Page titles

Features include

- complete catalogue listings,
  including book reviews and
  descriptions

- special monthly promotions

- information on NEW titles and
  BESTSELLING titles

- a secure shopping basket facility
  for on-line ordering

PLUS everything you need to know
about KOGAN PAGE

http://www.kogan-page.co.uk